SCALE

+ timbre

THE CHAN CENTRE FOR THE PERFORMING ARTS
BING THOM ARCHITECTS

VANCOUVER, BC

Neill Archer Roan

 forward by Arthur C Erickson

This book is dedicated to the Chan brothers, whose generosity and vision made the Chan Centre for the Performing Arts possible. Their love and respect for their father, Chan Shun, LL.D. 陳俊博士 – a modest but distinguished man, whose family and communities were immeasurably enriched by his wise example and generous heart – lives on in this extraordinary centre of art, education, and community.

THE UNMEDIATED EYE   Arthur C Erickson

I'm always discouraged about how little people see, even architects. Even those successful clients I've had who are major art collectors often see very little; one expects them to be sensitive to the visual, yet, all too often, they are not.

As human beings, we are so accustomed to looking at the world that we assume that we know how to see it. Many of us do not. You may be surprised that at times I count myself among the number who look but do not see. Actively seeing can be enormously tiring, discouraging, or even maddening, because the world is as full of vulgar and boorish visual language as it is of the written and spoken variety. To take

As a man is, so he sees. As the eye is formed, such are its powers.[1]

WILLIAM BLAKE

what is precious from the world requires seeing through a din of visual noise and effluvia. One indeed can learn to see. The rewards are enormous. To go beyond simply looking – to really see – requires a vigilant, disciplined consciousness – one that must be cultivated in practice.

This book – which undertakes the not inconsiderable task of revealing insight into Bing Thom's brilliant and ingenious Chan Centre – creates such an opportunity for practice. Bing's ability to execute with perfect understanding from the scribbles of a plan reveals an innate and marvelous ability to synthesize an extraordinarily complex and disparate set of elements into a coherent and powerful unity. I believe this ability emerges as much from his ability to see as from his architectural skill.

By looking at and reading this book about Bing Thom's Chan Centre, you will choose between looking and seeing. You will engage or not engage a number of modalities available to you: the emotional, the intuitive, the sensual, the instinctive, the intellectual. I urge you to exercise conscious choice-making in the use of these faculties, these "tools of seeing", so that you become aware of your process, and facile at more or less actively using them. Like all tools, some are better suited than others to particular disciplines and results.

The most important thing is not to think when you look. As much as possible, suppress your analytical self. Let your other responses dwell on it – your emotional, instinctual, sensual, and aural. Abandon analysis. This applies to any piece of art or architecture. You can't theorize if you want to understand at another level. Cultivate the direct response. Try not to judge or evaluate in order to prevent yourself from coming to a visual conclusion. You must take in as much as possible and judgment is a barrier.

Recognize that seeing is not a passive pursuit; it is an act of invention and like all actions, seeing requires exercise in order to be muscular. Much as we try, we cannot approach anything with an empty mind. Everything is derivative, even seeing. One approaches anything and everything with one's experience, knowledge, and memory. These things form the context in which we experience the direct response, which immediately and inalterably informs experience. A repertoire of experiences inevitably enriches one's ability to more richly experience the next.

Everything of value that I know has grown within me from my experience. After studying the history of architecture seriously, I traveled to various sites only to discover that the books and lectures were misleading. This was especially true of Greek architecture. In Athens' Parthenon, I encountered an aspect of energy that demonstrated contained vitality. The building is very much alive, but it doesn't move. It captures the aspect of a marvelous horse – arrested – wanting to move. It has this aspect because of the way it was built, which was not the way everyone assumes. The Parthenon was not conceived as some extraordinary application of mathematics and calculated proportion. It arose from the knowledge of the sculptor's hands.

I learned this after seeing the Parthenon when I traveled to Sicily where there are a number of unfinished Greek temples. At the temple of Segesta, some of the columns weren't finished. I discovered the piled up blocks, one on top of the other, were then sculpted out. It was the sculptor's eye – not the architect's – that created those columns. To my knowledge, we've never built that way again. Yet, this is one of the basic premises of Western architecture: contained vitality. Thankfully, it is impossible for me to see or experience any work of architecture outside the experiential context of my epiphany about the Parthenon. The experience enriched my ability to see everything since.

As we do not experience in a vacuum, we also do not see things in a vacuum. Learn to see beyond and around the object of your attention. All art and architecture inhabits space that contains other objects. These things, in concert, create

background and context that can be either disruptive or
complimentary. You will find that the background is just as
important as the object, itself.

For example, when an architect goes to an old city, or
to some hallowed place in a city to put in a modernist building,
historians and conservatory groups always want it to be in the
same style. Yet, some of the most successful transpositions
are radically different. In Nimes, France, next to a Roman temple,
Norman Foster put in an exquisite glass building. Rather than
detracting from the old temple, it enhances it. All too often,
the contemporary view of transposition is conciliatory. There is
an insistence on blending in by employing some similar elements
like temple columns. This inevitably decreases the value of
the experience rather than increasing it. It is inconceivable to
imagine looking at either the old Roman temple or its adjacent
glass building without experiencing the other as background.
To see one without the other is to miss the essence of
the experience.

On the whole, there is a great deficiency regarding the whole
aspect of relationships between buildings, objects, and works of
art. There are very few artists, when given an urban commission,
who take in the surroundings. Too many judgments are made in
isolation of the object or building, itself, and not how they relate

to each other. A dilemma of twentieth century culture is that we don't acknowledge the importance of relationship. Art must recognize this for nothing exists in a vacuum.

We must also recognize that we see within a cultural context: our own. But our own cultural context can and does restrain us from seeing within other cultural contexts. It can blind us if we let it. This was revealed to me when I first went to Japan in 1961. I was terribly frustrated by a very famous old teahouse located in the oldest garden in Kyoto. I found that this highly-respected work left me cold. I experienced the building as rather sad and retiring. It didn't thrust itself upon me. It withdrew. I found none of the physical vitality of Western architecture. It annoyed me and when I mentioned this to a friend, he said, "Arthur, you're just showing your ignorance."

This challenged me. I vowed to go back the next day, and stay until I fell in love with it.

I arrived first thing in the morning. Around noon, I was getting more and more upset at the arbitrariness of things. One column would be on a rock; another would be buried in the earth. Yet another would be on a log. There was no consistency. Exasperated, I gave up near lunchtime, and went and sat on a little viewing pavilion where a person invited to tea would wait until called. It overlooked the lake. I was sitting there; it was almost lunchtime, and I wondered "How can I get lunch without breaking my vow?"

I heard a rustling sound from one side of the pond. I looked, expecting monkeys. A group of women gardeners appeared working. Instead of using shears or saws, like gardeners or tree trimmers here in the West, they used nail scissors. What they were cutting were not branches, but single leaves of the maple tree. In the pines, they were trimming needle clusters and plucking off dead needles, one at a time. I said to myself, "This is ridiculous. How could this possibly affect the growth of the forest to achieve the overall aesthetic results that were obvious elsewhere?" After they had moved to another side of the pond, I examined the part of the garden that they had been through. It was a miracle. The forest suddenly was full of space. It was as if a wind had blown through and cleaned everything unnecessary out, leaving only what was essential. No Westerner could ever have done this, not knowing the nature of organic growth, only the muscular symmetry or grace of the human figure.

Afterwards, I returned to the teahouse, and found that all the contradictions I had disparaged in the little building were done to imitate or capture the spiral of natural growth. The organic form is always asymmetrical, trying to be symmetrical.

Nature is always in a frantic pursuit of perfection that it can never achieve. That pursuit conveys upon it the dynamism for growth. Nature's source of energy is frustrated perfection. Nature experiments with everything. No human could ever have invented a giraffe or a rhinoceros, only a divinity playing at the game of creation.

Then I saw that by founding columns on stone, logs, or the earth, they would begin a spiral movement up the whole structure, ending with the linear form of the pine branch extending out and lifting up its tips at the eaves of the building. This required a completely different way of evaluating what was seen.

At that point I experienced an insight into Japanese architecture that I had never had before. Western art is based on the human form which the Japanese have never shown interest in. Their art is based entirely on the depiction of nature – of rocks and trees and grass. The Japanese have words of judgment – like wabi, sabi, and shibui – that describe phenomena of nature that have no meaning to us. These phenomena typically represent aspects of loneliness, resignation, and an acceptance of mortality and the human cycle. Their contemplative impulse wells from a different spring than does ours in the West.

The fundamental aesthetic impulse – the muscular vitality of the human form versus the non-muscular grace of the plant form –

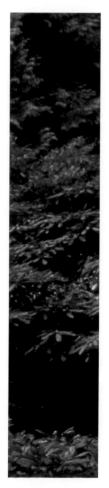

is culturally and contextually specific. What I had tried to see in Japanese architecture simply didn't exist as a basis for seeing and understanding their culture. I had to learn to see – as must everyone who wishes to actively see – in the power of cultural context.

Bing Thom's Chan Centre succeeds because it conceptually and executionally embraces many of the principals discussed above. The building respects and embraces its natural and cultural contexts. Acoustically and architecturally, the Chan is derivative in the best sense of the word – it builds and extends upon traditions, knowledge, and experience – even upon Bing's work with me on Roy Thompson Hall in Toronto. But like all projects of this scope, significant problems had to be solved over the course of bringing the building to fruition. Understanding the nature of these challenges and the working out of solutions increases one's appreciation of the results.

Originally, the University of British Columbia brought in a planner from Toronto who ignored the fact that the site did not exist on a perfectly flat and endless table, but rather on a piece of land that plunged into the forest and into the sea. The plan actually had the East and West malls continuing on one side right into the museum of anthropology, creating a semicircle that would have been fifty feet up in the air. This was a perfect example of theoretical planning that did not reference the site.

Sometimes theoretical planning creates magical effects; it can create excitement as with the city of San Francisco where steep grades cause streets to evaporate into the air. In this case, however, it would have been so much more beautiful had the plan recognized the reality of the sea and the hills.

Bing was faced with an original planning concept that was antipathetic to the site. His desire to preserve the forest directly conflicted with the planners' desire to remove all natural vestiges of the site, including both the slope and the natural growth of the original forest.

A view of the lobby from the forest

West elevation

The preservation and integration of the forest into the overall design scheme is one of the triumphs of the Centre. A site, itself, should always be a principal source of the design.

The basic difficulty, from Bing's point of view, would have been the approach from Marine Drive where the Chan Centre was to stand as the focal point of the university as one approached it. Therefore, he placed the concert hall super-structure over the theatre with its ancillary spaces in the forest. This solution created a very soft introduction of foliage to the forms of the theatre. The effect of the exaggerated verticality of the tower also made it an appealing icon for the university.

As one approaches the Chan from the mall surface, or from the parking garage – which is the usual approach, the scale of the building is reduced by its juxtaposition to a mature forest. By this device, Bing raises one's expectations immediately. It is further enhanced by the experience of looking into the forest through the Chan's great glass wall. It is a spectacular expression of the setting and a persuasive example of how a building must increase the experience of the setting rather than decrease it. From this very dramatic experience of Bing's sequence, one enters the warm, intimate, and intricate environment that he created for the pleasure of hearing music and experiencing theatre.

When one enters the Chan Shun Concert Hall, one is immediately struck by the warm embrace of the virginal wood interior. The experience is further enriched by the masterful expression of various functional devices of lighting and acoustics that are required for concert halls, for example the articulation of the vertical acoustical banners. There is a consistency of tone and color which unites the interior elements of the hall into a cohesive whole. Even the contrasting color of the seat fabrics is a deeper tone of the wood, itself.

Bing Thom's solution of the Chan Centre is masterfully resolved in terms of its detail. It represents the resolution of whatever challenge an architect has to confront and overcome in order to turn a space into a work of art. In this way, all the arts are similar – painting, writing, music, and architecture. One must achieve unity out of an indescribably complex set of requirements.

The magnificent acoustical reflector hovering over the stage, which is expressed as a chandelier, represents the continuation of an earlier idea at another scale – the ceiling in Roy Thompson Hall. When I first saw this expression, though Bing and I both worked on the chandelier design, I felt I was the original possessor of the idea. Seeing it transferred into the Chan, I had mixed emotions. I enjoyed and took pleasure in Bing

The main entrance

carrying my ideas and desires further; I felt honored by Bing doing that, but I also felt some faint possessiveness.

One can take any scientific or mechanical invention; somebody who originated the idea is envious of those who are able to take the idea further. The possessiveness or envy that is so natural to feel under these circumstances comes from the experience that these things are like one's children. In the purely selfish sense, it's not admirable that one has envy, but in the real sense, it's the way things happen. Ideas and expressions are absorbed and become part of a cultural expression that moves inextricably forward, beyond oneself.

As one grows older, one learns that one is often just an instrument in the development of civilization. There is a wonderful phrase by the Indian guru, Muktananda: "The divine is using creation and humanity, itself, to discover its own nature." I wonder both as I ponder my own work and Bing Thom's Chan Centre, what aspect of its own nature the divine has discovered through our work.

I suppose, it is in meditating upon this question, that I have renewed my passion for seeing. It has been through learning to see – exercising and cultivating a disciplined and intentional desire for the direct and unmediated response. More importantly – and to the point of this forward – I believe that by cultivating your ability to actively see, and by more vividly accessing your direct, unmediated response, you may discover more about your own nature.

The first balcony of the concert hall

COMING OF AGE   Neill Archer Roan

Can a building transform a community?

Evidence persuades that they can and do. Two high-profile North American examples are often cited here. New York's Lincoln Center turned a bedraggled, down-at-the-heels neighborhood into a cultural mecca as well as a thriving business, restaurant, and residential district. The construction of Washington's Kennedy Center helped fuel the transformation of the United States capital city from a sleepy cultural back-water into a cultural powerhouse.

What effects can they have on smaller cities? If the University of British Columbia's (UBC) Chan Centre for the

I would never have thought that one building, even one as significant as a performing arts centre, would have this kind of

incredible impact on a university community. It has transformed this university.

MARTHA PIPER, PRESIDENT, UNIVERSITY OF BRITISH COLUMBIA

Performing Arts is taken as an example, the impact has exceeded expectations and genuinely surprised both fans and critics alike. While the story isn't trumpeted in the worldwide media as in the cases of the Lincoln and Kennedy Centers, the relative impact is no less remarkable.

According to UBC's former and current Presidents, the Chan Centre has galvanized the university and its relationship with greater Vancouver. President Martha Piper underscores the point: "I would never have thought that one building, even one as significant as a performing arts centre, would have this kind of incredible impact on a university community. It has transformed this university." Former President David Strangway agrees: "I think the Chan Centre really succeeded far beyond my wildest dreams."

Nestled into a flowered and forested landscape at the ceremonial entrance of the University of British Columbia, the Chan Centre will celebrate the fifth anniversary of its opening in 2002. A centre of performing arts, university graduations and convocations, lectures, film, and gatherings, the complex thrives as a crossroads of community and university life.

"With most universities, you start with a great hall and then things happen around that", former UBC President David Strangway emphasizes. "These wonderful buildings that are

I LOVE TO TALK ABOUT WHAT THE CHAN CENTRE HAS DONE for our performing arts programs. The Chan Centre ensures that the very finest music students around the world are coming here to study because they know they can perform there. **Martha Piper**

so characteristic of campuses weren't built here [at UBC] because we were always scrambling to deal with the situation of the day. The need for a great hall had been evident for years. When I arrived at UBC, I described it as "The Unfinished Campus", Strangway recalls. "Now, every campus is unfinished, but this one was particularly unfinished in that there was no great hall. Graduation ceremonies were held in the gym."

"For decades, UBC was the only cultural institution in the province", Strangway explained. "The whole centre of things was around the creative and performing arts that are embedded in the University of British Columbia. We looked around and we realized that we did not have a suitable place for concerts and performances."

"We also had an opportunity to link with the community, because the community didn't have a small or medium-sized concert hall, either. The hall was always envisioned to be a facility that would be a place to be used by the community, too – a venue where the Vancouver Symphony, the Vancouver Recital Society, and other groups might perform in from time to time – as well as a place for our students to showcase their music."

The students and faculty, themselves, helped make the case. How does one ignore the needs of a music faculty capable of producing the celebrated opera artist Ben Heppner?

Ben Heppner • Choir • (next page) Main entry into The Chan Centre for the Performing Arts

BING THOM ARCHITECTS

The Chan Centre for the Performing Arts was designed by Bing Thom Architects (BTA) of Vancouver, BC. While the Centre is just one in a series of award-winning buildings produced by BTA, the Chan's international celebrity has earned Thom and his team plaudits from artists, architects, arts administrators, and critics, alike. New arts facility commissions in Washington, DC (Arena Stage) and China (Yuxi Performing Arts Centre) are under way as a result of the Chan Centre's many accolades.

Headquartered in Vancouver, British Columbia, Bing Thom Architects was founded in December of 1980, and is led by the award-winning Chinese-Canadian architect, Bing Wing Thom.

I love impossible projects. It's what I was born to do.

BING THOM

Born in Hong Kong, Bing Thom arrived in Canada as an eight-year-old boy, the youngest of three sons, speaking no English. A lifetime of hard-headed, single-minded striving began during his first month at elementary school in Kerrisdale where, as the only Asian in an all-white school, he fought with other kids on a daily basis. "I got a thick skin from that, and a thick head, too. Uphill battles are a part of my life." He often declares, "I love impossible projects. It's what I was born to do."[2]

Bing Thom radiates energy and youthfulness, perhaps because he swims vigorously every day. Decades of practicing daily transcendental meditation have conferred a ubiquitous calm upon his demeanor. Gliding through the maelstrom of his busy studio, Thom wears serenity like most men wear their skin. At least once a week, Thom sails alone on Vancouver's English Bay in his prized wooden sailboat – Sonija's Spirit – a racing craft that was designed by the legendary Gary Mull. Energetic and outgoing, Bing Thom is also an intensely private and contemplative man. Like the dialectic that has been his lifelong obsession and fascination, he is a thesis and antithesis working on synthesis.

Thom graduated from the University of British Columbia and the University of California at Berkeley (M. Arch), where he also lectured. He founded his firm after having worked eight years as a personnel and project director for the eminent Canadian architect, Arthur Erickson. Thom met Erickson at the University of British Columbia where he was Erickson's student for three years. While working for Erickson, Thom worked as a project director on several of Erickson's buildings, including Vancouver's Robson Square and Toronto's Roy Thompson Hall. Speaking from a lifelong fascination with Asia, Thom's former mentor, Arthur Erickson posits, "Originality is a Western notion, not an Asian one. There has never been a tradition of the individual there. Everyone contributes to the general culture and to the general development of knowledge; the individual contribution is submerged in the general, in the multiplicity of the group effort." This insight is of great assistance in understanding Bing Thom and his firm.

Thom's belief in team synergy – that the total is greater than the sum of its individual parts – reveals itself in the people with whom he has surrounded himself. "I am a collector of personalities and skills", Thom asserts. While most people at Bing Thom Architects are, in fact, architects, nobody is just an architect. The place teems with double- and triple-threat professionals. There are anthropologists, geologists, engineers, artists, construction managers, graphic designers, information technologists, electricians, landscapers, and biologists. The firm is culturally and geographically cosmopolitan, as well. An extraordinary number of languages are spoken by the firm's corps: Cantonese, Celtic, Danish, Dutch, English, Farsi, Filipino, French, German, Italian, Japanese, Mandarin, Pashtun, and Spanish, are examples.

Thom evinces loyalty and affection from his team. "Bing lets us really sing through our work", Clint Cuddington confided in a tone more characteristic of secret-telling than boasting. "We are better architects here because he grows us."

Though Thom unquestionably tends the rudder of his firm, he entrusts its management and operations to a team of three managing directors: Michael Heeney, Luciano Zago, and Arno Matis.

A reserved and softspoken man, Michael Heeney has been with Thom the longest of the three. Thom recruited Heeney for his strengths in architectural design and urban land economics. Heeney served as Project Director for the Chan Centre, and for many of the firm's projects over the last decade, as well. His design and management expertise soon propelled him upward, his judgment honed by years of design and development both within and without the firm.

Luciano Zago came to BTA to work as a design architect having had considerable experience in theatre design. Like

Thom and Heeney, Zago was educated in architecture at the University of British Columbia. He was responsible for the design and development of the Chan Centre's public spaces, and invented the innovative system suspending the catwalks and concert hall ceiling – the fret-string system. Zago is admired by his teammates for his warm and flexible style, and is expert at managing large project teams, and in representing the firm to clients.

Arno Matis' self-effacing style obscures an astute, Harvard-educated entrepreneur who, among other pursuits, has developed a side business in information technology. Matis worked as a project designer for the Chan Centre. Matis' marketing savvy, experience in construction management, and wide-ranging design experience combine to make him an invaluable member of the team.

Bing Thom · Michael Heeney · Luciano Zago · Arno Matis

PLANNING, PROGRAM AND CONSTRUCTION

It is a long, tiring, and treacherous journey from deciding
to build a new arts complex to creating a detailed set of plans
to build it. If one builds a science building, one builds for
scientists; if one builds an arts building, one builds for artists
and artists tend to have big imaginations. Big imaginations
spawn big visions; big visions draw big questions like picnics
draw ants. Every big question has a thousand little questions
standing in queue behind it, all clamoring for attention. What
will it be used for? Where will it be? Who will use it? Who
is its audience? Addressing these questions is akin to gazing
into a hall of mirrors; eternity unfolds before you.

Most people don't realize that concert halls are more technically complicated than hospitals.

BING THOM

If an institution's ability to envision doesn't outpace its resources, then it probably doesn't think big enough. Most institutions' eyes are bigger than their stomachs. When the vision has to be translated into a program, some furrowed-brow, rolled-up-shirt sleeve-working group is charged with the tedious, but unavoidable task of paring back the vision so that the program fits within budget constraints.

Even if it were explicitly intended to do so, it is unlikely that a process could be better designed to fracture trust or bruise relationships. First, the need is sold. Second, people are asked to unfetter their imagination, think big, and dream. Third, all the ideas are written down, usually on big flip charts. Pride in ownership takes root. And – as is human nature's bent – a request for advice is heard as a promise to take it. Predictably, many ideas – often the boldest and most memorable – cannot help but fall victim to the budget axe. Yet, in the scores of ideas generated, there is innovation that informs development and clarifies priorities.

Processes that are more sensitive to managing stakeholder expectations would likely go a long way towards diminishing the price paid in social capital. Still, feelings and relationships aside, a bold visioning process endows generously. Most successful planning and development strategies need one.

Detail of the chevron roof

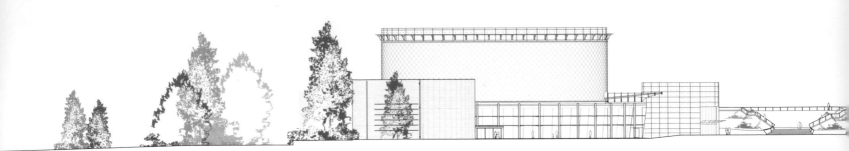

North elevation

Even then, there are surprises.

"This was almost ten years ago, now. As different departments and users started talking about requirements, our two consultants, Donnell Cost Consultants (the project's early cost consultants) and Theatre Projects (the program consultants) were clicking away on their laptops. Sure enough, on Sunday afternoon, out spit the numbers. We found out that what the users wanted was $60 Million plus. The budget, at that time, was $14 Million or so. At that point," said Heeney, "the project was put in abeyance while the university went back and re-jigged the program and the budget."

For Bing Thom Architects, the budget planning and program development processes were problematic. UBC directly engaged Theatre Projects Consultants to develop the program, eliminating the benefits usually bestowed by interplay and mutual accountability between architect and program developer. There was virtually no communication between the architect and program consultants during the reprogramming phase, a period of nearly a year. "We were not involved in developing the budget," Heeney said, "which I think was a fatal flaw in the program and the way the university administered it. We were given the program and budget as a fait accompli when we started up again."

Though BTA was out of the loop, UBC was adept at juggling its needs, its means, its donor's intent, and the program's scope. Planning officials scrutinized master-planning documents for ways to achieve some economies of scale. Facility development funds that had previously been set aside for both the film and theatre departments were transferred to the project budget. Both the design program and ability to pay for it reflected the change.

The revised program reflected a need for spaces to accommodate theatre, film, concerts, and opera/musical theatre. Though there was broad consensus that dedicated spaces were required for both film and theatre, there was still considerable debate about whether one hall could reasonably accommodate concerts, opera, and musical theatre.

Initially, plans called for building a single facility – a multi-purpose performing arts space often referred to as a "lyric theatre". But, after an exhaustive period of visiting other facilities and consulting experts, university officials concluded that building a dual-purpose hall was inadvisable. Though advances in technology have since addressed most concerns about dual-purpose halls, UBC reasoned that they must reject flexibility for quality.

"It became obvious after a while that we should not compromise", Strangway said. "The experts said 'You can't have acoustical excellence in a proscenium-type concert hall.'"

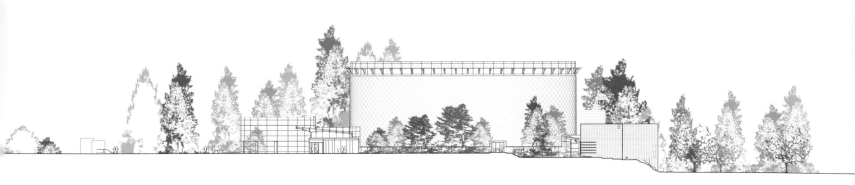

South elevation

As an option, the university began to discuss two separate facilities in order to meet opera/musical theatre program needs. Strangway insists that two separate halls were never planned, but were an alternative scenario that had to be explored. As responsive administrators, they wished to respond to the needs of their faculty and students.

"I don't think that anybody thought that we were looking at a $60 Million project", Strangway insisted. "The conclusion was that to build a whole-scale proscenium-type theatre plus a whole-scale concert hall was going to be twice as much. Our preliminary work indicated that we could build a project in the $25 to $35 Million range. We had to choose one or the other. We could not afford two separate halls." Finally, the university chose to build a dedicated concert hall. There was a certain irony in the decision; it was the UBC musical theatre production of *Sweeney Todd* – not a concert – that boosted early efforts to build the centre.

One difficulty in developing a large project with an institutional client the size of a university is the sheer number of people, agencies, and regulators one must satisfy. Committees, trustees, faculty, staff, donors, independent consultants, the list seems endless. Eventually, communication channels are established and chaos is reined in. Fortunately, for the Chan project's benefit,

Don Paterson became such a channel. "Don Paterson was invaluable", Bing Thom affirms.

A Professor of Economics and former Associate Dean of the Faculty of Arts, Don Paterson was tapped to represent the university's interests. A warm, thoughtful, and atypically loquacious Scot, Paterson's thrift, doggedness, and unwavering devotion to the university's students made him the right man for the job. Keeping people informed, prioritizing, controlling costs and moving things along wasn't for the faint of heart. Even Paterson was occasionally disheartened.

"I didn't ever lose hope that something would be produced. However, I got pessimistic from time to time that it would be of a quality that we would all be proud of", Paterson reminisced. "At times, we had to make compromises with respect to the architectural nature of the building, but one of the wonderful things about the project was that each of us reached our pessimism at different times. There was never any sense that the project was ill-fated or doomed. There were times, however, when we all had to sit down and do some serious hard thinking." Paterson's hard thinking was highly-valued by President Strangway who wanted the Faculty of Arts' needs met, and trusted Paterson to keep their interests in mind.

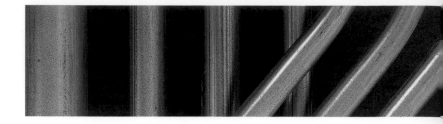

"It was very important that the Faculty of Arts be fully engaged in the Chan's development because the outcome was going to have to suit their needs as well as the broader community needs", Strangway observed. "Don Paterson and Bob Kubicek were incredibly facilitative and Don, in particular, spent a lot of time with the project management people and Bing. When issues like the lobby size or seat quality came up, Don was the person who came back to me and said, 'I've looked at this from all different perspectives.' He's not a construction guy but he sure came to understand what the issues are and how various trade-offs had to be made. Don took a very, very hands-on, pragmatic approach."

One of the proposed trade-offs involved the choice of seating in the Concert Hall. The fight to contain costs was a constant struggle. In one move, project managers decided to replace planned fabric and wood seating with classroom seating.

Horrified, the BTA team temporarily installed a row of the contemplated classroom seats in the concert hall, and then demonstrated the dismal effect. Incredulous, Zago, challenged Paterson and the university's project managers, "You have spent all this money on creating the finest acoustics and now, are you going to put in chairs that squeak when people shift in them?"

Paterson could not abide that choice. He requested an immediate meeting with the President where he refuted the penny-wise, pound-foolishness of installing squeaky seats in a concert hall. Strangway was convinced; he intervened immediately to preserve the original seating.

When Bing Thom's team heard that the large Canadian construction firm Ellis Don had been chosen to build the Chan Centre, they were pleased. The firm had a significant track record in successfully building complex cultural facilities, especially in Eastern Canada. Alarms sounded, however, when the firm's project directors and site architects discovered that the crew that would be building the Chan was comparatively inexperienced. The buildings' drum-like form was to make it a challenging project for any crew, let alone a green one.

Typically, at an early phase of construction, a concrete quality standard is established. When BTA Project Architects inspected the benchmark pour, they were underwhelmed. "We almost made them tear it down and start over." Zago said. "From that day on, the concrete pour was always excellent."

"The bottom line", Michael Heeney retorted, "is that the hall is very beautiful and you've got to give Ellis Don credit. In the end they had a very good concrete crew; the people they had were true craftsmen."

There is no substitute for great craftsmen when building a concert hall. One of the regrettable casualties of our time is that some extraordinary craft skills are dying along with the aged artisans who possess them. Hand-plasterers, for example, are an endangered craft species. Since few buildings employ this building method now, the demand for the skill is low.

Very thick plaster work is prized by acousticians. Its density reflects sound energy beautifully. In the upper reaches of the Chan's concert hall, covering the technical gallery, is a very thick layer of plaster.

Gallagher Brothers, an old Vancouver family company, were selected as the drywall contractor. Since the company's current generation of artisans lacked heavy hand-plastering expertise themselves, they brought people out of retirement. They assembled their fathers, grandfathers, uncles, and great uncles to help do the plaster work. In what amounted to a working family reunion in overalls, they painstakingly and lovingly plastered the concert hall ceiling.

Zago recalled, "All these old guys were sixty feet up in the air on scaffolds having a fantastic time teaching the younger men how to do the work. It was beautiful."

"They had a lot of fun doing something that ordinarily would have been quite difficult to do," Heeney replied. "If you had to build a building like this ten years from now, you would have a hard time. You wouldn't have that skill set."

Detail of the web of electrical conduits

THE SITE

When Bing Thom began wrestling early on with what the Chan Centre would become – what its essence might be, and how it would spring from its time and place – he found it very difficult to focus on the building. An evergreen forest, thicketed with sixty-to-eighty-year-old rhododendrons and azaleas, stood in the way.

"This performing arts centre was supposed to sit in the middle of this very beautiful forest. Within the forest there were about 200 rhododendrons and azaleas. It was a very sensitive site – a lovely garden – and I was supposed to clear the site for this building. I was quite unhappy with the prospect for a number of reasons", Thom remembered.

A forest bird never wants a cage.[3]

"Aside from taking the trees down, the sheer size of the building would be so out of scale with the rest of the area, Thom asserted. "I knew that our project would be eight or nine storeys, yet surrounding the area were quite low-scale buildings, only three or four storeys high. I tried for awhile to explain to the university that other sites should be considered. I tried to place it within or adjacent to some taller buildings."

Before Bing Thom had been engaged to design the Chan Centre, an extensive campus-wide planning process occurred. The immense thousand-acre campus – approximately the same size as downtown Vancouver's footprint – had been exhaustively examined by university officials, faculty, and planning consultants. Concern about the campus continuing to sprawl outwards escalated. The university's leadership wished to use the Centre's placement as a tool to help densify the campus.

Located adjacent to the ceremonial entrance to the University of British Columbia – Flag Plaza – the site had been promised to the project's principal donors, the Chan family. Tom Chan, who led the family's effort to bring the Chan Centre about, remembers that, "having this building located at Flag Plaza was quite important to my family – physically and symbolically –

because it's located at the border between the community and the university."

After being told that other site options were out of the question, Thom mulled over his predicament. "Even though they told me, 'You've got to put the building on this site', I didn't want to chop down the trees. This forest was originally an experiment planted by some early professors in the university's forestry department. There were a variety of trees in this forest that were significant to the history of British Columbia."

Consternation became inspiration. Thom turned to his friend and colleague, the eminent landscape architect Cornelia Oberlander, who persuaded Thom to rethink the forest's relationship to the building. Thom realized that "you can always design a concert hall or a performing arts centre in an urban setting. Seldom do you have a forest setting. Why not play up the forest? Why not light the forest at night so that when you come out of the concert hall, you actually feel you're in a forest? I realized that this would be quite a unique experience." university planning and development officials had other ideas; they thought the forest a hindrance rather than an enhancement to the site.

"There is a fantastic view of the mountains", Thom mentioned. "The university wanted me to chop the trees down to get this view from the Chan. I explained that, even if you take the trees down, the mountains are dark at night, when most people would experience the view. But, if you light the trees, you will have a foreground that can become a stage set to the building. Once we finally agreed on the fate of the forest, we set about surveying every tree. In the end, we planted the building around each and every tree. We protected the trees during excavation because we knew that we would be disrupting the root structure and changing the water table. In the end, we cut down one tree because it was in the middle of the road. Otherwise, we didn't disturb one evergreen."

"We moved all 200 azaleas and rhododendrons offsite into the university nursery. These plants were priceless because some of them were 60 to 80 years old; you couldn't buy them for all the money in the world. I was able to use these plants as a foil to the building, especially in concealing the loading dock and the mechanical and emergency electrical generators."

The azaleas and rhododendrons would not be the only foil to the building. Many trees within the forest had grown higher than 100 feet. To make the building seem smaller, Thom decided to nestle the building into the forest by sinking the structure down into the ground as far as possible. As a result, the eight or nine storey building rose only six storeys, partially solving the scaling problem.

1   Marine Drive
2   Forest
3   Chan Shun Concert Hall
4   Telus Theatre
5   Royal Bank Cinema
6   Entry Foyer
7   Flag Plaza
    (pre-development)

Aerial view with site plan overlay • View of Point Grey with inset of UBC site location

DESIGN

The sheer massiveness of the Chan Centre was one of the most difficult design issues that Bing Thom faced. "I had to find a way to make the building look smaller," remembers Thom, "especially on such a sensitive site".

In addition to nesting the building into the site escarpment, Thom settled on the idea of employing curves in his overall design strategy. The curvilinear design was augmented by applying zinc panels to the complex exterior. Designed in a "fish-scale" pattern, the panels exaggerate one's sense of the wall disappearing into the distance as it recedes. The zinc's soft gray patina creates, as well, a misty, other-worldly effect where the

In designing a building, there are layers of discovery. Each time you come to a building, it's like a good book or a good piece of music; it doesn't matter that you read or hear it ten times, twenty times or more. Each time you discover in a fresh way. You see in a fresh way. That is what a good piece of architecture is about.

BING THOM

sky's color – whether blue or cloudy gray – is gauzily reflected on the panel surface.

Thom's final design strategy to reduce the mass of the Chan's size involved creating a "corona" that rings the top of the concert hall drum. During the day, the corona catches sunlight from above, casting soft shadows onto the zinc; it glows like a halo. At night the corona glows with captured ambient light from the building below, stopping the eye from looking to the top of the wall which disappears into the night.

The sublime forecourt is one of the most powerful spaces in the Centre's design. It is the point of ingress, of meeting, and of departure. It is a place of enclosure by landscape, yet openness to sky. The sense of place is created by both man and by nature.

A forecourt or "clearing within the forest" was created which set apart the building's ceremonial entry from the axis of the University's Main Mall. This strategy is aesthetically in keeping with the Japanese concept of "ma" space – a space which simultaneously separates and joins, creating a pause or threshold from one realm to another.

As a result, on a beautiful summer evening, one can stroll across the space admiring the hand laid stone comprising the retaining walls, and gaze upwards at majestic hundred foot

Detail of corona

cedars and firs. In Spring, the rhododendrons' glorious colors transfix the eye with their waxy luminescence. During a Vancouver rainy winter evening, a quick dash across the forecourt is rewarded by a slightly breathless arrival into the foyer's warmth and light.

The Chan Centre was conceived as four distinct buildings, built of either poured concrete or solid masonry blocks. These large drum-shaped buildings anchor the complex; the public and support spaces flow between them. These "linking spaces" are built of contrasting, light steel structural framing and glass wall enclosures.

As one passes through the foyer, past the coat check and ticket office – under the chevron shaped roof – one enters the Chan's breathtaking lobby. One is immediately confronted by Gordon Smith's painting, *Silent Woods*, a work commissioned by Tom Chan. It captures the essence of the winter forest, blending landscape and architecture – amplifying a sense of interior infinity.

Months earlier, in the dead of winter, Smith, Chan, and Thom drove out to the dark, unheated site to get a sense of the painting's effect. They set up a projector some distance from the wall where the painting would be hung, and projected a dim ghost of the painting on the lobby wall. Though the image struggled on concrete reflection, it was apparent that the painting captured the winter forest.

Artist Gordon Smith and Tom Chan • Night view of the lobby

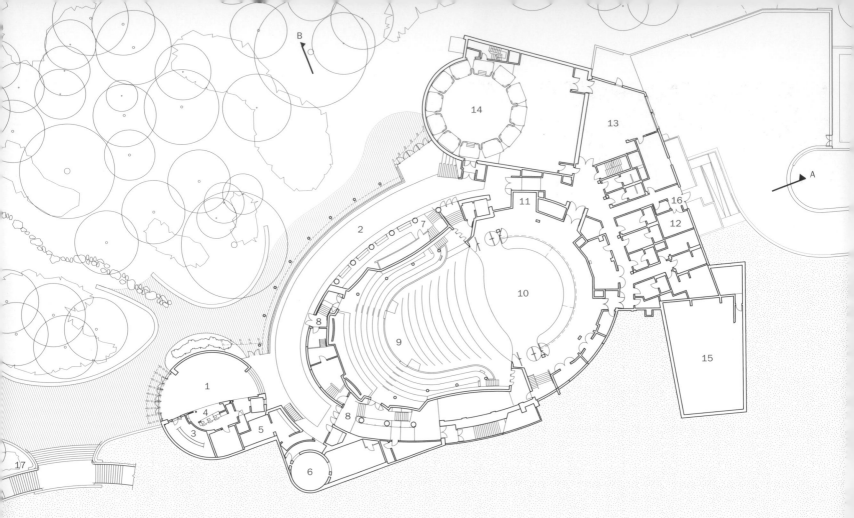

Forest level

1	Foyer	5	Men's WC
2	Lobby	6	Women's WC
3	Coats	7	Concession
4	Ticket Office	8	Sound + Light Lock

9	Chan Shun Concert Hall
10	Stage Area
11	Instrument Storage
12	Dressing Rooms

13	Loading + Receiving
14	Telus Theatre
15	Cinema Above
16	Stage Door

17 Parkade
For building sections see page 56

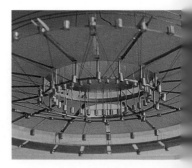

STUDY MODELS

Forecourt entrance   Concert hall   Acoustic canopy

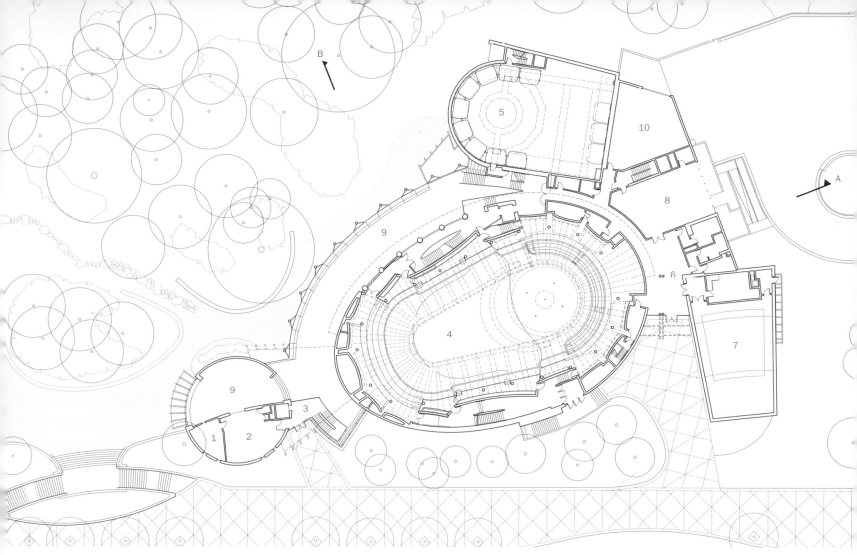

Plaza level

1   Director's Office
2   Administration
3   Administration Entry

4   Chan Shun Concert Hall
5   Telus Theatre
6   Cinema Lobby

7   Cinema
8   Great Performer's Lounge
9   Open to Below

10 Electrical Room
For building sections see page 57

Lobby glazing options

Foyer form

Lobby structural model

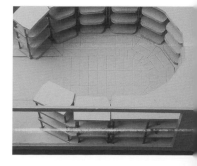

Theatre model

Another dimension of infinity exudes from the magnificent exterior glass wall of the lobby that opens onto the Chan's forested setting. It is no accident that the glass wall appears so transparent as to be virtually invisible. Lighting designer Bill Lam and Bing Thom journeyed one evening into the forest, armed with panes of glass and flashlights, to determine the perfect angle to build the lobby's glass wall. They wanted to ensure that someone looking out into the forest would never see their own reflection, whether day or night. The much-reduced lobby size, which was cut due to budget constraints, was saved by that glass wall design. "Because

it is curved", explains Thom, "one never senses the finite edge of the space. There is a sense of infinity, a sense of exploration and discovery."

Though Bing Thom laments the compromise he was forced to make in reducing the lobby's size, Arthur Erickson finds serendipity. "In Vancouver, the forced intimacy, created by the constrained lobby is good", Erickson asserts. "We need to be forced into social situations that contrast with the dispersed way in which we live on the mountainsides, canyons, and shores. The design creates intimacy that we instinctively abhor in the way we live, striving for isolation."

Thom and Zago conceived the lobby as a place of incidents, compared to more ceremonially defined spaces. To heighten the sensation of chance encounter, they created a relaxed geometry that allows – even encourages – forms and people to collide with each other. For example, between the Telus Theatre and the Concert Hall, the two drums pinch the lobby space. Inserted into the space between them is a sculptural staircase linking the upper and lower lobbies. The stair is skewed in the space, its geometry influenced by the straight wall of the theatre on one side and the curved wall of the concert hall on the other.

(previous page) Interior view of lobby and sloping glass • Stairway from plaza entry into lobby

THE DESIGN OF A PERFORMING ARTS CENTRE encapsulates everything I love and believe about architecture. Like music, a building must always respond to human emotional needs, especially our yearning for the next surprise or the next delight. Bing Thom

I HAVE ALWAYS LOVED the Artur Schnabel quote, Thom said, "The notes I handle no better than many pianists. But the pauses between the notes – ah, that is where the art resides."[4] In architecture, the pauses between the notes are soft incidental spaces that provide transition between larger utilitarian spaces. Bing Thom

A view from the foyer to the lobby beyond · Detail of railing · Upper concert hall stair · Lobby

If one seeks a litmus test for an architect's attention to detail, don't evaluate based on a building's façade or grand lobby. Inspect the washrooms. They demonstrate passion about how a building is habituated.

A theatre or concert hall redoubles the challenge. Theatricality, sense of event, and mood determine success. At the same time, practical considerations like size, flow, light, and access must be considered. Practically, performing arts facility washrooms must reasonably accommodate a large volume of people in the space of an intermission that ranges from fifteen to twenty minutes. Surprisingly, an architect's grasp of women's washroom needs is often the subject of indignant allegations of insensitivity or worse.

The women's washroom at the Chan Centre is one of the building's most popular spaces, evincing jokes about male washroom envy. Inset into a circular steel and green glass pedestal, the bank of sinks encourages conversation and mutual appraisals. The sink – conceptually based on a communal font – helps make handwashing a ritual pleasure. After washing, a patron need only spin on her heel to glance into any of a circle of mirrors mounted on the room's wall, for a quick makeup check.

Women's washroom

Thom's yearning to surprise and delight is apparent in the way he and Zago anticipated the experience of the individual entering the Chan Centre. Expectations are heightened as one moves through a series of compressions and expansions of space until finally experiencing the expansive bloom of the performance spaces.

"We were always playing with scale in the project", Thom explained, "creating transitions of scale for the perceiver. You come out of the garage – an enclosed space – then you enter the lower plaza which is an open space. Then, scale is compressed again when you come into the foyer, which is a

A view from the lobby towards the foyer

smaller, closed space. From there, you enter the lobby, and though it is a relatively small lobby it feels like a large space for two reasons: its curved glass walls open to the forest outside, disguising the size; and the lobby's curved glass walls evoke a sense of infinity. Then you go into the sound and light lock, another transitional tight space. Finally, you enter the hall, which is actually an intimate room. But, it feels like a huge room because you have come from a space that was very compressed and tight."

"The series of transitions, the flow of spaces from open to closed to open to closed create an element of surprise through a series of transitions. In the end, it is delight in this experience of the building that makes people love the building. A series of transitions from large to small or open to closed are like crescendos (becoming gradually louder) and diminuendos (becoming gradually softer) that make turning a musical phrase artistry." It is those transitional spaces that Bing Thom uses to craft the "architectural phrase".

At the climax of Thom's architectural phrase, resounding like a sforzando – an emphatic and sudden musical accent – are the Chan's two principal performance spaces: the Chan Shun Concert Hall and the Telus Theatre. Their designs are driven by their respective intended uses, the Chan Shun is a dedicated concert hall for music and the Telus was created for theatre.

An exterior view of the sloping glass wall of the lobby • Lobby • Stairway up to plaza entry

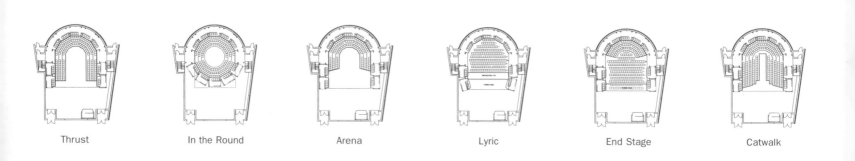

| Thrust | In the Round | Arena | Lyric | End Stage | Catwalk |

The Telus Theatre was conceived as a "working and teaching space", a down-and-dirty, rough-and-tumble black box to be used by both students and faculty in UBC's Theatre Department. Inspired by Shakespeare's fabled Globe Theatre in London, twelve tri-level, movable audience towers can be configured in more than a dozen settings, depending on a production's design. The configuration chosen determines the number of audience seats, ranging between 100 and 275. All twelve towers can be moved to the space's end to create an empty room within which to work. The theatre is one of the most popular sites among location scouts looking for movie- and television-making spaces.

A third space, the 158-seat Royal Bank Cinema was designed for UBC's Film Department, and is seldom used for public events. Designed for screenings, lectures, and small film festivals, the room, though comfortable, is utilitarian in its design and furnishings.

Thom understood early on that the heart of the complex would inevitably be the Concert Hall – a room that he knew must simultaneously evoke sensations that are usually experienced as polar opposites. The hall must feel intimate, yet grand. Comfortable, but formal. Thom believed that the hall must willingly yield every emotion, sensation, memory, or allusion

Examples of flexible audience seating and stage configurations • Telus Theatre interior

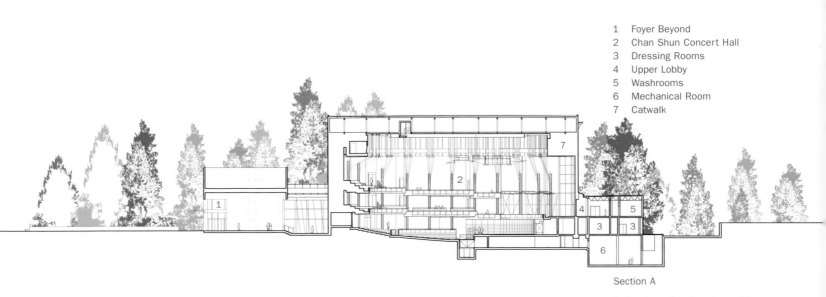

1 Foyer Beyond
2 Chan Shun Concert Hall
3 Dressing Rooms
4 Upper Lobby
5 Washrooms
6 Mechanical Room
7 Catwalk

Section A

A view from the plaza toward the concert hall. *For site plan see page 40*

that an artist on its stage might try to evoke – a range of artistic possibilities that is mind-boggling to contemplate. As a practical matter, he knew, by contemporary standards, that the room would be relatively small, but it had to feel big.

Inspiring performers to give their best was very much on Bing Thom's mind when he designed the Chan Shun Concert Hall. As aware as Thom was about the bracing psychological impact of warm reverberation returning to a performer's ear, the team sought – through design – to reinforce what the ear would hear with what the eye would see. Bing Thom calls this strategy "visual acoustics".

"Visual acoustics are about a room not only being full, but feeling full; not only being intimate, but being grand, as well. An imaginative and skillful use of colors and materials creates this effect. For example, we know that many musicians like the idea of having wood near them because wood lends a sense of warmth Creating a sense of visual warmth is very important to a performer. It's a part of inspiring them to play well. In that first instant, the artist must feel inspired and uplifted by the room", Thom explains.

Shape and lighting have an impact, also. "The hall has a violin-like shape – and though an artist may not be immediately conscious of this – I believe he or she senses it", speculates

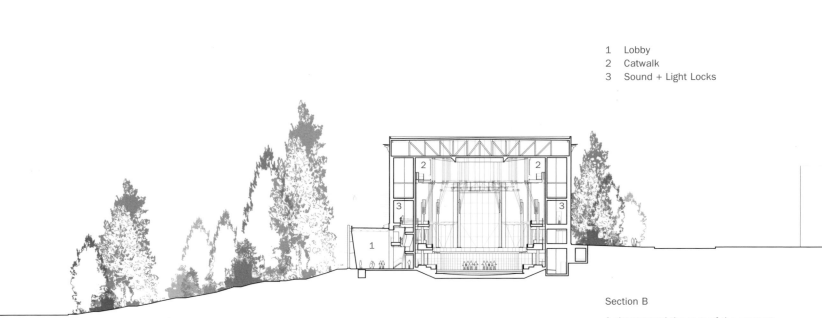

1 Lobby
2 Catwalk
3 Sound + Light Locks

Section B

A view toward the rear of the concert hall. *For site plan see page 41*

Thom. "Also, the curvature of the balcony fronts and the sense of closeness that the curvilinear shape creates is important. The shape and the light create a sensation from the stage that the balconies hover over the audience. The reflected light on the faces of the audience in the balconies' front rows increases intimacy. Plus, vertically stacking the audience up on different balconies is helpful because if there isn't a full house, it doesn't show because the rear rows aren't visible. You get that sense of enclosure very quickly."

Concert halls require some ambient light because people want to look at their programs. Artists also want to be able to see their audiences in order to gauge their reaction to the performance. Recalling a bygone era when candles flickered from balcony fronts, the architects placed light sconces on the maple balcony facades to create ambient light. "These sconces provide that little bit of twinkle to increase warmth and intimacy," Thom said. "It's very subtle. Each sconce has a shield which reflects the light back onto the wood which then reflects it again onto peoples' faces. It's just enough light to highlight the balcony shape and give the artist a sense that there is an audience out there."

Floating high above the stage and the audience is a 37-tonne acoustical canopy, all powered by one 1/2 horsepower motor

(next pages) Detail of an head anchor • Chan Shun Concert Hall

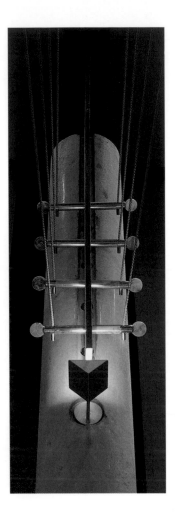

because it's all so perfectly balanced. Typically this element is treated as a part of the ceiling and appears visually heavy. In this case, however, the physically heavy canopy is made to appear light by treating it as a chandelier, making it the hall's principal decorative element. Juxtaposed against golds, silvers, beiges, and wood, the acoustical canopy attracts blissful audience gazes like some strand of precious pearls ringing a graceful neck.

The elliptical geometry of the concert hall ceiling is reinforced by a series of radiating stainless steel cables that support the lighting catwalk at the ceiling. These cables are expressed as a series of "frets" and "strings" which reinforce one's visual experience of being inside a musical instrument. Their form, inspired by the heads of violins and 'cellos, the frets are made up of an interplay of stainless steel cables with brass fittings. Halogen spot lighting rakes through the frets and strings, across the blonde wood and plaster-paneled surfaces, and creates a geometry of reflection and shadows that lend detail to the blonde wood and plaster surfaces.

Here one sees Thom's philosophy regarding function and beauty played out in the firm's approach to design. The intricately decorative fret-string system also supports the ceiling and catwalks. The precisely detailed finish schemes of the poured concrete structure create pattern and rhythm while comprising the complex's bones and muscle. It is nearly impossible to see where function ends and beauty begins, because in the firm's design approach, there is no difference between beauty and function.

Bing Thom insists that "beauty and functionality are never in conflict. What works and what is beautiful are one and the same thing. Beauty is not something applied to something else. Beauty evolves from a deep understanding of need."

I THOUGHT I was in heaven. **Kyung Wha Chung, violinist**

FORM AND ACOUSTICS

It is puzzling in this era of moonshots, cloned creatures, virtual reality, and other feats of modern technology that achieving consistently good concert acoustics remains so dicey. Everyone, it seems, waits anxiously to hear the first strains of music in the new hall to judge the ultimate success or failure of their acoustical aspirations.

ARTEC's Russ Johnson, one of the world's foremost acousticians and the acoustical designer of many of the world's greatest concert halls – including the Chan Centre – ruminates, "Regarding acoustics, there is no end to the lessons to be learned. The way that the materials of the room, the dimensions

Within the span of ten minutes, we move from highly amplified music to totally acoustic music. At one moment, we might want to sound like we are in the Taj Majal, and the next moment we might want to sound like we're in a music club in downtown San Francisco. I remember feeling that the Chan Centre seemed like every aspect of sound had really been thought about. You have the sense when you are there that everything you are going to be feeling and hearing and seeing on stage has been attended to. That is rare. Very rare.

DAVID HARRINGTON, ARTISTIC DIRECTOR, KRONOS QUARTET

of the room, the shape of the room, [and] the way that the architectural envelope creates the sound in the room is so complicated and so complex that it is quite possible that the world will end before all of the mysteries are solved."

Among the myriad design components that most effectively shape the intensity and quality of a hall's sound, Johnson cites five pivotal considerations: the shape of the hall's architectural envelope; the number of seats installed in the hall; the inclusion of side balconies; installation of a moving overhead sound reflector or canopy; and systems of moving fabric.

Though the Chan's concert hall is reminiscent of a violin's shape, Russ Johnson says that "It has the basic aspect of a shoe box", a shape that repeatedly emerges throughout Johnson's concert hall designs throughout the world, from Birmingham to Singapore. "For me", Johnson emphasizes, "the important components of a shoe box are the ceiling and the central sections of the side walls. In the rooms we design, we often maintain the shoe box shape throughout the room." The hall's floor also features a grade that slopes slightly up.

"The single most important initial consideration when designing an opera house or concert hall is the seat count",

Detail of the parterre facia

Johnson underscored. "The loss of sound energy comes primarily from the sound absorption of people's clothing, not just in the cubage of the room. To get a full sound, a sound with power, strength, and presence is the basic goal of good acoustics. When you have a tremendously large audience area, that just essentially kills off the sound." Undoubtedly, at a time when so many halls with 2,500 seats or more are being built – primarily for ticket-revenue-generating considerations – the fact that the Chan's main concert hall has just 1,400 seats is an essential factor in its success.

"We worked very, very hard to make the room as small as possible", Luciano Zago recalled. "We had to balance maintaining the seat count with designing the volume of the space to be as small as possible."

"Sometimes, you're bound to measure less than a quarter of an inch or a half an inch just to make sure you've got enough space", Bing Thom explained. "You have to be quite diligent to make sure you're not overworking – being too cautious – and making the room bigger than it has to be or under-sizing the room only to find out you're losing seats. To completely redo and resize the room is a lot of work just to get an extra ten seats."

"A very, very important part of achieving clarity in the Chan was the use of side tiers", Johnson affirmed. "The sound comes up off the stage hits the side tiers and the undersides of the side tiers, and is reflected back down to the main floor. This design strategy prevents the middle of the hall from being starved of the sound energy that creates immediacy or presence." Additionally, large-radius convex-curved panels were placed behind each balcony section to reflect and diffuse sound energy smoothly throughout the main floor area. The concert hall's interior walls, which are all exposed concrete aggregate, were bush-hammered (a small handheld jack-hammer) after the concrete was poured to provide diffusion of mid-and very high-frequency sound.

Musicians have always known that a great instrument improves a great performer. Can anyone imagine wishing for anything less than a Stradivarius in Itzhak Perlman's hands? Great halls improve performers, too. Leila Getz, the Vancouver Recital Society's Executive Director, believes that Vancouver audiences get better performances from artists who appear at the Chan than audiences who hear the same artists in other halls. "Because it's so wonderful acoustically, the artist's level of playing and performance have to live up to the Chan's acoustics. The acoustics make for more musically expressive possibilities."

In one way, a concert hall is like a musical instrument; it is prized or discounted according to one very subjective, but very tangible criterion: is the sound beautiful?

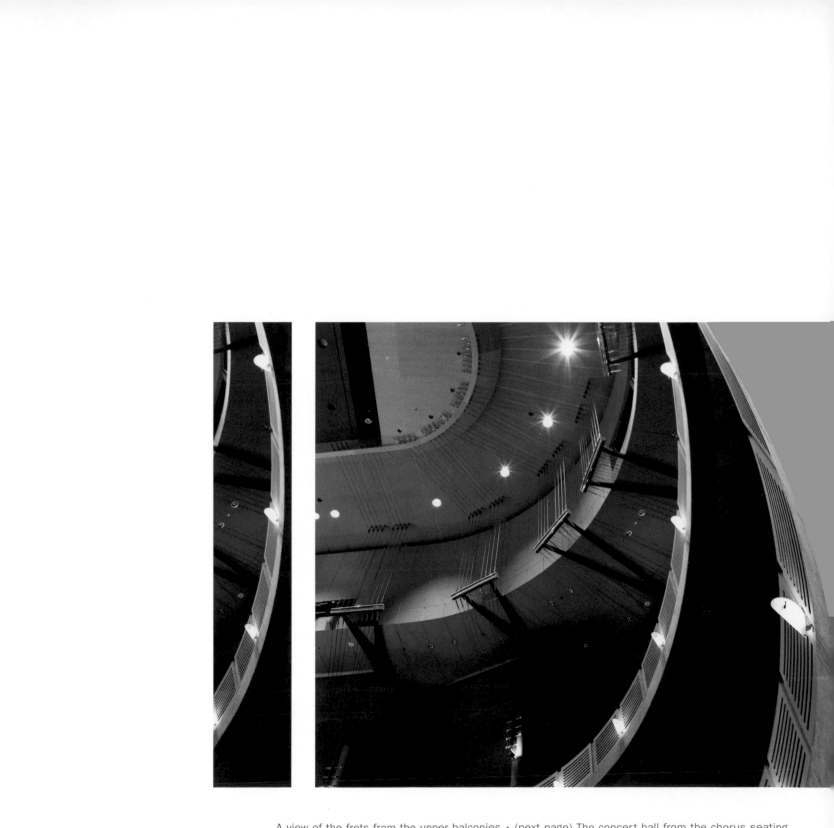

A view of the frets from the upper balconies • (next page) The concert hall from the chorus seating

Beautiful sound, Johnson opines, calls for two dimensions of quality that – for hundreds of years – have been considered mutually incompatible: clarity and reverberation. "Conductors, particularly, have always been saying the same thing, over and over. The words they use are sometimes different, but what they all say is 'I want simultaneous bloom and clarity.' I knew from studies I had done that these parameters are inherently antithetical", Johnson said. "If you take a concert hall or an opera house of the sort that has been built during the past three or four hundred years, as the clarity increases the reverberant quality fades and vice versa. Creating both is a tremendous challenge. When it came to achieving this magical quality of having both clarity and presence simultaneously, I didn't really understand at the outset as I managed to do it."

Like nearly all concert halls, the Chan Centre may house the whispering musings of a Renaissance lutenist one night, the rambunctious declamations of a brass quintet on another, and the lush, rhapsodic sweep of a symphony orchestra on yet another. Perhaps unreasonably, but undoubtedly, each of these musicians and – more resolutely their audiences – expect that the hall will adapt to the performance of the moment – and reveal it to perfect advantage. A tall order, indeed, but an order that was recognized as having been filled during the Chan's Opening Night Festivities when Peter Maxwell Davies' oratorio *Job* was given its world premiere performance.

"The tone was rich, warm and full, as kind to instrumental blasts at their loudest as it was to tiny details and human breaths of pianissimo sound", reported Lloyd Dykk in a review of the opening night performance.[5] Given the differences in tone, volume, and in repertoire between a harpsichord at one extreme and a brass band at the other, how can any one room succeed with such extreme acoustic demands?

A computer-controlled-and-motorized curtain system, a 37-tonne adjustable acoustic canopy, and an ability to change the acoustic properties of the stage's rear wall within the Chan

CREATING A SENSE OF VISUAL WARMTH

is very important to a performer. In that first instant, the artist must feel inspired and uplifted by the room. **Bing Thom**

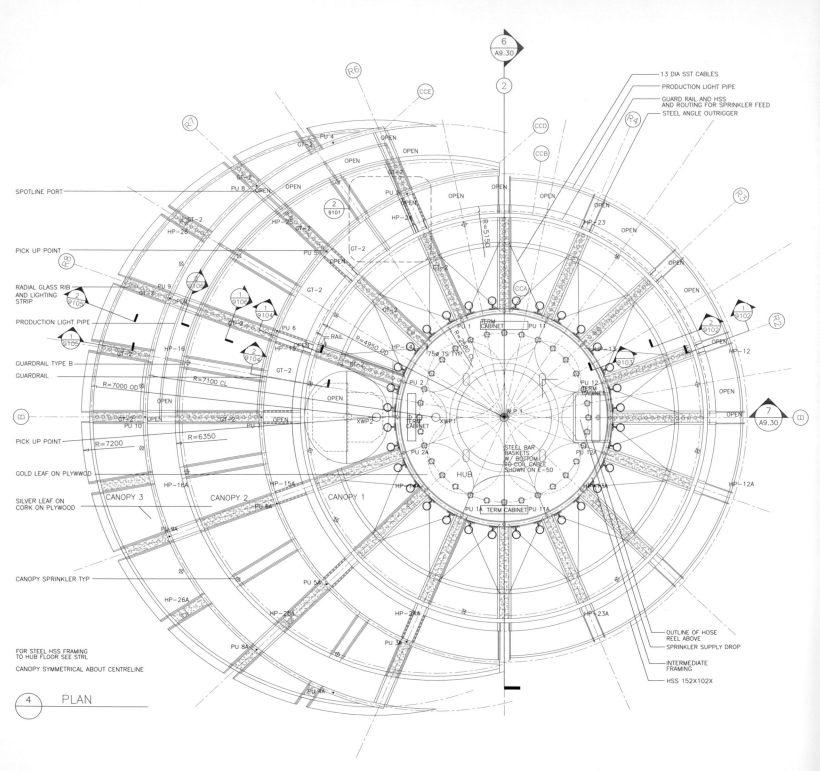

SPOTLINE PORT

PICK UP POINT

RADIAL GLASS RIB
AND LIGHTING
STRIP

PRODUCTION LIGHT PIPE

GUARDRAIL TYPE B
GUARDRAIL

PICK UP POINT

GOLD LEAF ON PLYWWOD

SILVER LEAF ON
CORK ON PLYWOOD

CANOPY SPRINKLER TYP

FOR STEEL HSS FRAMING
TO HUB FLOOR SEE STRL

CANOPY SYMMETRICAL ABOUT CENTRELINE

13 DIA SST CABLES
PRODUCTION LIGHT PIPE
GUARD RAIL AND HSS
AND ROUTING FOR SPRINKLER FEED
STEEL ANGLE OUTRIGGER

OUTLINE OF HOSE
REEL ABOVE
SPRINKLER SUPPLY DROP

INTERMEDIATE
FRAMING

HSS 152X102X

CANOPY 3   CANOPY 2   CANOPY 1

HUB

W.P.1

STEEL BAR
BASKETS
W/ BOTTOM
TO COIL CABLE
SHOWN ON E-50

④ PLAN

makes a rather wide range of acoustical adjustments possible. The stage's rear walls are comprised of woven Maple wood panels that are acoustically transparent. The panels conceal large solid doors which may be opened or closed to decrease or increase reflections of sound energy from the stage. Opening the doors causes energy to leak backwards; closing them positions a solid, dense surface that efficiently bounces the energy forward towards the audience, increasing presence. Where the sound absorptive textures of greater or lesser volumes of fabric can help dampen too much reverberation, adjusting the canopy closer to the source of sound can help amplify a softer instrument's volume, lending it more presence and making artistic nuances more audible. In order to precisely create those nuances, musicians must be able to hear each other.

For a musician on stage, perhaps nothing is so unnerving as not being able to hear other musicians with whom one is performing. Ensemble – the quality of nuanced precision that musicians co-create – is a defining hallmark of musical greatness. It is also nigh impossible to achieve in a hall where one cannot adequately hear one's colleagues.

"Musicians hear themselves through the floor", Thom said. "It's like the head of a drum – a vibrating membrane. To achieve

Detail plan of the acoustic canopy • The acoustic canopy under construction • (next page) Canopy

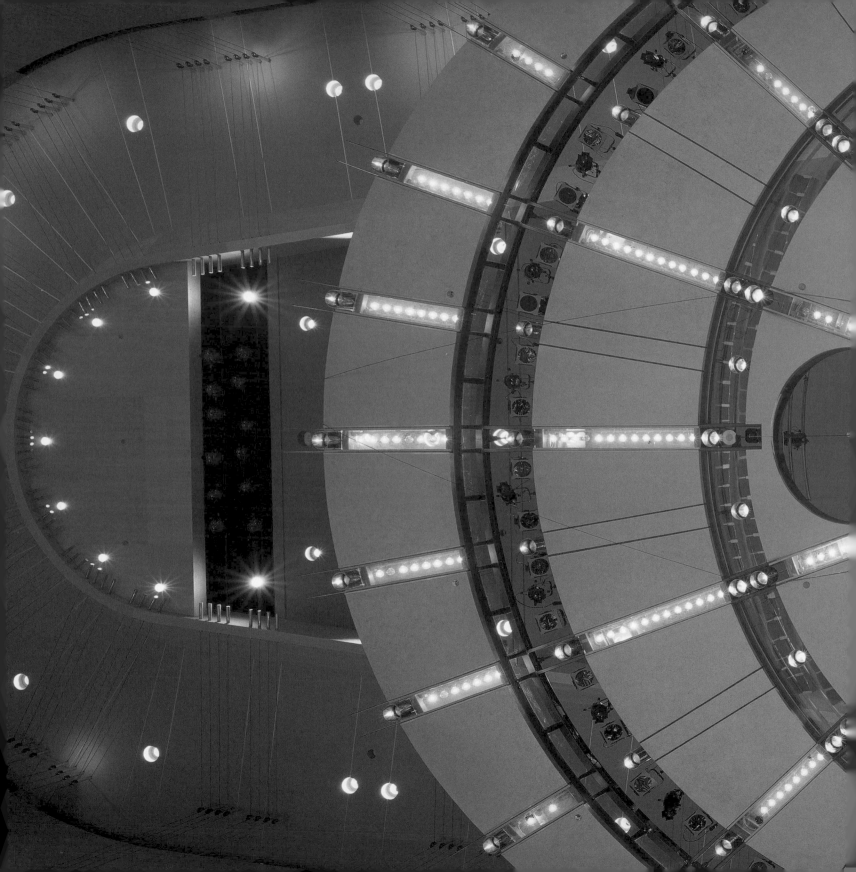

this, the floor has to be sprung, acoustically. The floor is actually floated on neoprene gaskets so that it vibrates with the musical resonance created in the room."

Adjustable reverberation within the concert hall is one of the features that makes the Chan desirable, no matter the style or period of performance. For example, cathedral sound – particularly desirable for antiphonal choirs performing Palestrina – would irretrievably muddy a Beethoven piano quartet if the hall's reverb could not be dampened.

Using curtains which are constructed of two layers of very heavy fabric with six inches of air space between the layers, the reverberative properties of the room can be adjusted between a range of 2.75 seconds (curtains concealed) to 4.5 seconds (curtains exposed).[6]

During the 2000 Festival Vancouver, the Chan's acoustical potential to recreate cathedral-like sound was tested. Two of eleven concerts were performances of vespers: Monteverdi's *Vespers of 1610* and Rachmaninoff's *All-Night Vigil*. The curtain system was completely concealed and the canopy was raised to its highest position. Chan Centre Director Michael Noon remembers well the result: "The audience commented on just phenomenal sound." Likewise, Lloyd Dykk, Music Critic of the Vancouver Sun wrote, "Ideally it would be heard in a church with various spaces able to rarefy its antiphons and echoing spatial effects, but splendour still rang out in the acoustics of the Chan."[7]

Though it may seem like they spring fully-formed and self-contained from the minds of their architects and the muscles of their construction crews, concert halls – like people – have their progenitors. As E B White wrote in 1937, "Heredity is a strong factor, even in architecture."[8]

When Johnson contemplated a shape for the Chan Centre's concert hall, he drew inspiration from older and much-venerated concert halls. Revealed in their shapes, features, finishes, or spaces – concert halls reflect both what is known and what is suspected about what makes these mysterious structures work. It is as if the accumulated knowledge and craft, art and science combine and recombine to form a building's "DNA" where "what's worked before" are the stem cells that are capable of morphing into any of the thousands of concepts or components that comprise a finished structure.

If one were able to pry the roof off the Chan Centre's Chan Shun Concert Hall and gaze downwards from a great height – so distant that seats, stage, and boxes became texture instead of detail – one would see the elegant concave and convex curves of a violin's shape. Johnson insists that the violin's shape did not influence his thinking. Rather, the success of earlier halls using

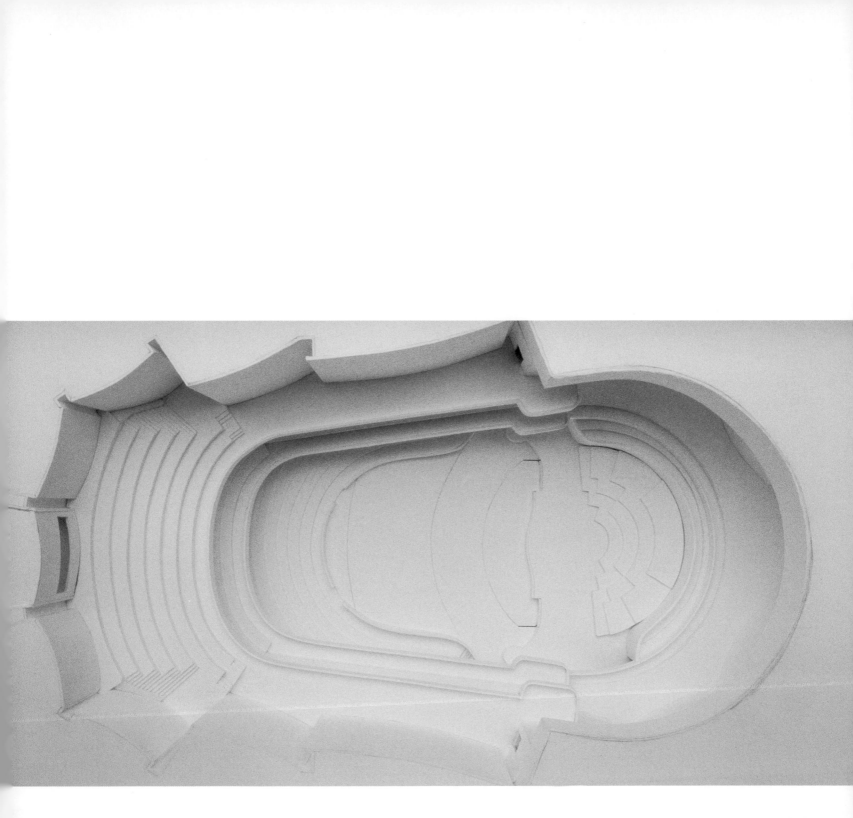

The initial acoustician's model of the concert hall

that same scheme drove his design. "It (the shape) has nothing to do with a violin. If you look at a lot of the old halls from around 1850 to 1890, they had this shape. One is the concert hall at the top of the Troy Savings Bank in Troy, New York and another one is the Academy of Music in Philadelphia. If you look at those two halls, you will see that both of them have that shape."

Johnson's use of the Troy Savings Bank Music Hall as an acoustical model for the Chan Centre makes sense. Broadly recognized as an acoustical gem, the hall has been used to record many of the CDs published under the Dorian label. Since it was opened in 1875, a pantheon of musical giants have appeared there including Rachmaninoff, Paderewski, Iturbi, Szell, Horowitz, and Rubenstein, among many others, most of them extravagantly complimenting the hall's beautiful sound. Beautiful sound begins with its antithesis: silence.

In 1896, Belgian author Maurice Maeterlinck wrote that "Silence is the element in which great things fashion themselves." This is particularly true with concert halls.

Great silence is rare in our noise-polluted environment. Noise levels that might pass for an acceptable level of silence in everyday living would never pass muster with Thom or Johnson. Even the noise caused by the movement of air was carefully

considered in their design. "Keeping the movement of heated or cooled air very slow was important", Luciano Zago affirmed. "The air ducts below the Chan Centre are so large that you can walk upright within them. These large ducts provide for sufficient air volume to move through the Chan slowly, but more important, silently." Fostering silence by avoiding noise is one strategy; isolating sound is another.

Each room of the Chan Centre is acoustically isolated from every other room. They are separated by acoustical isolation joints – two-inch-thick pieces of neoprene rubber that run right down to the building's footings. Piping, conduits, and mechanical

systems are all suspended on little springs in order to isolate and dampen any vibrations running through the structure which might transmit sound into performance spaces. Additionally, double walls with dead air spaces between them arrest noise from leaking in from outdoors or from other spaces within the Chan Centre. Surprisingly, something as trivial as a screwdriver dropped between walls, then forgotten, can defeat months of planning and design – not to mention millions of dollars invested in achieving silence.

"We were very careful to have senior architects Lynn Pilon and Earl Briggs on site to inspect all the acoustical joints

Detail of the concert hall ceiling

and walls. When you have these acoustical joints, if they're not perfectly isolated, then the acoustics are compromised. It is important to make sure that there are no workmen carelessly dropping a Coke can or a tool between the walls which might bridge the gaps; the wall spaces must be absolutely clean and clear", Thom explained.

Pilon's and Briggs' fastidious and precise work, according to Thom, was "extraordinary and invaluable. The standards that Lynn and Earl enforced during the project's design and construction are one of the reasons that the building is so successful. They made a big difference", Thom remembers.

Just as something that shouldn't be there and is can compromise acoustical quality, something that should be there and isn't can also work against good sound. "On the inside of the hall – wherever there is wood – the wood must be bonded to the concrete very, very solidly. If the glue is not applied properly and there is empty space between wood and concrete, when the sound hits it, there is not a solid reflection. This causes an energy loss in the room." Other properties of wall surfaces affect acoustical properties as well.

"When they bid the job, the contractors didn't realize just how rough the surface had to be inside the concert hall to refract the sound", Michael Heeney, the Chan's project director recalls.

"We had given them a sample wall surface specification at the Vancouver Aquarium. We asked the contractors to go and visit, but they never did. In the end – on a rotating weekly basis – one guy with a little jackhammer had to jackhammer three quarters of an inch into the entire surface of that concert hall."

Heeney recalled the contractor's displeasure at having to resurface such a massive volume of concrete wall: "They missed this in their quote so they were quite reticent to do it. Because there was so much concrete, no one person could possibly do it all. It would kill him or drive him nuts."

In the end, several workers took turns. But Heeney – with a detail-orientation typical of his firm's culture – worried that the wall's rough patina might not be consistent because so many different workman would jack-hammer the concrete. "There was no particular patina, depending on who jackhammered. One guy would have a strong right arm and another wouldn't. Fortunately, in the end, there were enough different people doing it that we got sort of a general pattern."

It is mind-boggling to imagine a collaboration that requires thousands or even hundreds of decisions in pursuit of something so ephemeral as conjuring a successful concert hall. When asked to break down those parts of his collaboration with Bing Thom that led to success, Johnson balked. "There is no way to

break it down", insists Johnson, "It's very simple. Bing and I really, truly collaborated. It was not a pretense. It was not a hollow use of the word. We really did work together and the two of us created the acoustics of the room. Every square foot of the concert hall, every square foot of the ceiling, and every square foot of the walls and the floors, all the dimensions – everything – that's where the acoustics are created. This was a true collaboration where Bing took my basic design and turned it into a magical piece of architecture."

Former ARTEC executive Bob Wolfe, summed it up: "Bing Thom's a complete joy to work with and likewise his staff."

Thom has an intensely process-driven explanation for his ability to juggle the endless barrage of considerations, decisions, changes, and confabulations necessary to succeed. "We build tons and tons of models", he said. "We put ourselves constantly in the place of the performers. We put ourselves constantly in the place of the audience. We never trust the drawings."

As good as the Chan Centre's acoustics have proven to be, as the old saying goes, "you don't have to be sick to get better." The Chan's concert hall, like any instrument, has a host of untapped artistic possibilities yet to be coaxed into regular use. "We are working right now, with Bing and with the Chan Foundation, to teach ourselves more about the acoustics of the Chan over the next two or three years. We will learn more about how various adjustable features affect the sound of the room. We will undoubtedly improve the situation for the audiences at the Chan because we will be passing that knowledge on to the staff that operate the Chan on a day-by-day basis", predicted Johnson. It will only get better.

Detail of the balcony ceiling · Side tier box · A view of the upper lobby mezzanine · The upper sound and light lock · Curtain and anchor head detail

THE LIFE OF THE CHAN CENTRE TODAY

If one wanted to make a movie portraying the world's richest man, what would his house look like? Producers grappled with that question while working on Director Peter Howitt's MGM thriller, Anti-Trust, a film that drew its inspiration from the recent anti-trust case brought against mega-corporation Microsoft by the United States Justice Department. When location scouts looked for a house that "Gary Winston" – the character based on tech-czar Bill Gates – might order built, they settled on architect Bing Thom's Chan Centre for the Performing Arts.

The Chan Centre admirably acquitted itself. The film's art directors used the Chan Centre's elegant exterior to showcase the

People say a library is the heart of a university. Well, maybe the Chan Centre's the soul of this university.

MARTHA PIPER

tech-czar Winston's taste and intelligence. Because the Chan's spare lines and sculptural contours soar, so must the quality of Winston's thinking. It was used because it was persuasive "packaging" for what Winston – the technology icon – must be.

While it's not unusual in the rarified world of movie-making that a building is used to set the stage for a story, it is unusual for the building to have been commissioned and built by a publicly-owned Canadian university. These are institutions that take pride and pains in their frugality. The Chan Centre was the lowest cost performing arts facility constructed in North America at the time of its opening, as measured on a per-seat basis –

the normative measure for comparison. However, when one confronts the difficulty involved in arranging time to use the Chan, it might be enough to discourage Mr. Gates, himself, let alone a movie producer. The place goes round the clock.

A day doesn't go by that the Chan Centre isn't occupied by one of its many users. Concerts, plays, rehearsals, lectures, graduations, seminars, symposia, recitals, and films incessantly occupy the new facility. university and community jostle for time. There is a relentless quality to the frequency of events, not unlike Vancouver's maritime weather – some new front is always coming in.

The Chan Centre's founding Director, Michael Noon juggles the Chan Centre's agenda. He must balance the academic needs of UBC's Faculty of Arts with a beseeching Vancouver classical music community clamoring to expand its use of the Chan. Noon must also manage to keep the Centre's budget ink black. Noon's budget-balancing act has been eased by an unanticipated, but much-welcomed, by-product of the Chan's design. Nobody guessed that the Chan would generate so much rental revenue from television, film, and commercial producers looking for a distinctive setting. While many facilities confront annual deficits, Noon has succeeded despite receiving a modest subsidy doled out sparingly by the the University of British Columbia.

Reserved and thoughtful, Noon is an architect by training, a bureaucrat by experience, and the Chan Centre's Director by passion. The Chan's widely-acclaimed acoustical success was not to surprise Noon: "I expected it to be as good as it is. Theatre design is my forte and I had the feeling it would be wonderful before we opened."

"I'm at the end of my career", Noon reflected, "and to have been the person who opened the Chan Centre and programmed it and run it for the last five years; I can't think of a more emotionally and professionally satisfying crowning part of a career in the performing arts. It has a lot to do with the Chan family and their

love of what the Chan Centre represents, especially their continued interest. I find this most humbling, most extraordinary. It's been more valuable than anything else I've done in my life."

While Noon wasn't involved in the design and development process, he commented on design issues he discovered after he arrived – just in time for groundbreaking – and improved some service areas, particularly the Chan's ticket office design.

One would imagine that awe of the place would wear off given enough experience. But, after nearly five years of working day-in, day-out in the Chan, one still hears affection for the Centre creep into Noon's voice, like when he described being a part of the audience himself: "Last night I heard the VSO (Vancouver Symphony Orchestra) with Judy Kang play the Mendelssohn violin concerto. It wasn't the most fabulous performance, but I felt close to the music. I think: 'It can't be any better.' The materials and the relationship of stage to audience is perfect. I say that as an audience member watching the audience. I also say it as a performer looking out at the audience. There is an intimacy that has to do with the design of the hall."

Martha Piper's connection to the Chan Centre is personal. On September 25, 1997, Piper was installed as the 11th President of the University of British Columbia. "I was overwhelmed", Piper recalls. "It is indelibly imprinted in my can give its students — especially some of its tremendously gifted students — access to such a fine, fine facility. Donald Paterson, **Professor of Economics**

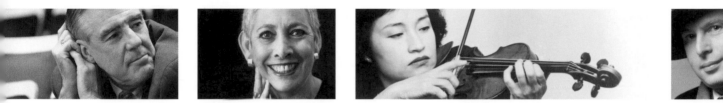

memory that I was fortunate enough to have this very personal experience take place in such an incredible facility."

An American by birth, but a Canadian by choice, Martha Piper radiates vigor. Exuding the kind of gravitas that all too often eludes attractive and energetic women, Piper is reputedly a skilled fundraiser and advocate. She speaks passionately about the value education brings to academic and community life.

Piper came to UBC from the University of Alberta and McGill. One expects a university president to have impeccable academic credentials, so Piper's previous experience as a dean and vice president aren't particularly surprising. However, handing out "Think About It" baseball caps at her installation along with her exhortation to "outhustle the competition" set an "on-the-move" tone to her nascent presidency.[9]

"To me, the Chan Centre represents what we're trying to achieve at UBC," underscored Piper. "It set the stage for our vision, for my own thinking about what we should be doing at the university in reaching out to the community, in trying to bring people together, in interactive learning, in trying to make big small. All of those things that we're grappling with at the university are embodied in what the Chan represents."

Unquestionably, the Chan Centre has become renown first and foremost as a performing arts centre. "It has promoted the university in a major way", reminds Michael Noon. "Everybody wants to play at the Chan. What the university doesn't take enough credit for, in addition to performing arts events, are the international conferences, the twenty or more high school graduations, and the CBC recording sessions", Noon said.

President Piper couldn't agree more. "The Char Centre is more, in my mind, than just a wonderful performing arts centre. While that's a primary role – one that we honor – it's also a place where people come to learn, engage in dialogue, and create a sense of community."

Piper has a strong vision of how university communities ought to be interacting. In her view, interaction advances learning. Both students and faculty must be able to both speak and be heard. Piper believes that facility design has driven the way learning has traditionally taken place and she sees the Chan loves learning interaction.

"When people say to me, 'You can't have interactive learning with big groups' – it all has to be twenty students – I always say, 'No, go into the Chan Centre. Somebody can stand up in the middle of that hall and express themselves, and everyone can hear.' It's an amazing facility, not just for performing arts, but for the interaction that goes on in a university community."

Martha Piper • David Strangway • Michael Noon • Leila Getz • Kyung Wha Chung • András Schiff • (next page) Ben Heppner in concert

Sir Peter Maxwell Davies, composer
Marc-André Hamelin, piano
Qiu Xia He, pipa
Timothy Findlay, author
Veronica Tennant, dancer
Quartetto Gelato
Tafelmusik w/ Jeanne Lamon, conductor
I Solisti Veneti Chamber Orchestra
Christopher Parkening, classical guitar
Spirit of the West
John MacLachlan Gray, author, composer
Judy Kang, violin
Nancy Hermiston, soprano
I Musici De Montreal
The Count Basie Orchestra
Ben Heppner, tenor
St. Lawrence String Quartet
Naomi Wolf, author, feminist
Herbie Hancock and Wayne Shorter, jazz piano and saxophone
European Union Chamber Orchestra
Angelika Kirchschlager, mezzo-soprano
w/ Jean-Yves Thibaudet, piano
Inti-Illimani

Gilbert Kalish, piano
Arditti String Quartet
Voices-Relyea
Jane Coop, piano
Maureen Forrester, contralto w/ David Warrack, piano
Kronos Quartet
The Peking Acrobats
Israel Camerata Orchestra
Guher and Suher Pekinel, duo piano
Moscow Chamber Orchestra

Irakere
Chucho Valdés Quartet
Midori, violin w/ Robert McDonald, piano
Rita Constanzi, harp
The Canadian Brass
The King's Singers
Amadeus Trio
Joe Sealy, composer, actor, music director
Rita MacNeil, vocalist, songwriter
Les Violons du Roy
Harlem Spiritual Ensemble
Pepe Romero, classical guitar

Leif Ove Andsnes, piano
André LaPlante, piano
Academy of St. Martin in the Fields
Yefim Bronfman, piano
Gil Shaham, violin w/ Akira Eguchi, piano
Steven Isserlis, cello w/ Stephen Hough, piano
The Beethoven Trio Vienna
The Juilliard String Quartet
Glenn Miller Orchestra
Jamie Parker, piano
Patricia Shih, violin
Andrew Dawes, violin
Angèle Dubeau, violin
Rivka Golani, viola
Amanda Forsyth, cello
Joel Quarrington, bass
James Campbell, clarinet
Martin Hackleman, French horn
George Zukerman, bassoon
Angela Cheng, piano
Robert McDuffie violin, Yoon Kwon violin,
w/ Charles Abramovic, piano

Estonian Chamber Choir w/ Tallinn Chamber
Orchestra Tõnu Kaljuste, conductor
Yin Cheng Zong, piano
Richard Goode, piano
Lara St. John, violin
Henri-Paul Sicsic, piano
Canadian World Music Orchestra
Barbara Bonney, soprano w/ Caren Levine, piano
Zakir Hussain, percussion
Bustan Abraham
St. Lawrence String Quartet
Penderecki String Quartet
Exaudi Chamber Choir
Schafer Quartet Project
Tommy Dorsey Orchestra
Stephen Hough, piano
Anton Nel, piano
Nicholas Kitchen, violin
Yeesun Kim, cello
Tasmanian Symphony Orchestra
w/ David Porcelijn, conductor w/ Liwei Qin, cello
Emanuel Ax, piano
Ben Heppner, tenor
Preservation Hall Jazz Band
Tedung Agung Ubud, gamelan ensemble

David Daniels, counter-tenor
w/ Martin Katz, piano
Vienna Boys Choir
Ian Wright, TV Personality ("The Lonely Planet")
Paragon Ragtime Orchestra
w/ Rick Benjamin, conductor
Kyung-Wha Chung, violin w/ Itmar Golan, piano
International Sejong Soloists w/ Leon Fleisher,
piano w/ Hyo Kang, artistic director

The Chan Shun Concert Hall Timeline of Notable Performers

IN THE BEGINNING

"Tell the president that he will not be disappointed", Chan Shun said through his son, Tom, who interpreted for him. Four men rose from their seats overlooking Hong Kong and warmly shook hands. Fifteen years later, those words still ring resonantly in Strangway's memory. No, he was not disappointed nor would he be.

At that time, David Strangway had been President of the University of British Columbia for two of the twelve years he would eventually serve. Engaged in the largest fundraising campaign for a university in the history of Canada, Strangway was to preside over an unprecedented $880 Million of

We are responsible for passing on good things and better opportunities to the next generation.

TOM CHAN, PRESIDENT, CHAN FOUNDATION OF CANADA

construction and expansion during his tenure. The Chan Centre for the Performing Arts was to be the jewel in the crown of the university's transformation from a provincial university to one deserving national stature.

It was 1987 when David Strangway accompanied Gordon Campbell – Vancouver's former Mayor and, at that time, future British Columbia Premier – on a courtesy call to the Chan family enterprise's Hong Kong headquarters. They were engaged on a promotional mission for Vancouver and had decided to visit the Chan family after having come to know the brothers Tom and Caleb Chan in Vancouver.

During the meeting Strangway recalled, "We talked a lot about Vancouver and what Vancouver was all about. One of the messages in this conversation, which was relayed through Tom, was basically that Vancouver is a very unusual city. It is a city that – probably better than anywhere else in the world – has integrated different communities, different societies, and different races in a way that has not exploded as it has in other parts of the world. A lot of the conversation was about what it was that made Vancouver so special as a place that was very racially diverse, and yet at the same time, had an awful lot of tolerance."

Exterior detail of lobby and foyer • The Royal Bank Cinema entry

Living in a racially-diverse city where tolerance was practiced was important to the Chan family at the time, given a recent decision to move their family and fortune to Canada. Asian immigration to British Columbia was not altogether non-controversial in the late 1980s.

"As the conversation moved on", Strangway said, "we had within our mission plan the view that we needed to develop a major complex on the campus. The complex was to have three parts: the concert hall that is there; the studio theatre that is also there; and a studio facility for artists and painters. We also had conversations about whether they would like to consider helping us with a new library, which was also part of our mission plan."

At the time of the meeting, the Chan family had lived in Vancouver for less than a year. However, the family patriarch, Chan Shun, had come to Vancouver during the late 60s with one of his oldest and closest friends, David Lam, a man who had served as one of British Columbia's most popular Lieutenant Governors during the late 80s and early 90s.

"David Lam was one of my father's best friends when they were first trying to establish themselves as businessmen", Tom Chan explained. "We relied on him because he had lived here so long whereas we were recent immigrants." Though the Chans were well known to UBC officials prior to formally meeting,

David Lam formally introduced the Chans to the university. Chan remembers that the prospective performing arts centre was just one of a number of projects that were discussed during the meeting. "We asked, 'What are the long term needs of the university?' This was one that stood out strongly from our perspective. We almost immediately liked the idea."

When the Chans made their gift for what would become the Chan Centre for the Performing Arts, it was then the largest gift to a cultural institution in Canada's history. Given the wide array of needs and competing priorities in British Columbia, when asked, "Why a performing arts centre?" Tom Chan replied with a laser-like response: "It goes back to what we wanted to do. We wanted to be able to cater to an educational mission as well as the community's well-being. Doing something like this would cater to the enjoyment of both."

"At that time, although my father was retired", Chan said, "he was very interested in motivating people to make things happen. Although my brother and I were very involved in running the business and were well-established, we still looked to our father for his wisdom. We always felt he was a very special Christian businessman with a strong philosophy and values in life. We still rely on those values for guidance. We discussed it and thought: 'We have always supported education. Let's think

MY FATHER ALWAYS TAUGHT US the example of Abraham in the Bible. Abraham built his altar and made his thanksgiving to God immediately upon arriving at a new village every time. He did not wait until he had made his gain before giving it back. Certainly, at the time, nine years ago, some friends advised us to wait until we had made money in Canada before making this major pledge. We believe that charity is about the worthiness of the cause, and not for the benefit of the donor. Our commitment to UBC's 'World of Opportunity' campaign was not simply an opportunity to help a great university. It was an opportunity to make a very personal statement of faith about our gratefulness to God to have new opportunities in a 'new world', and to continue to be his good stewards.[10]

Tom Chan

Chan Shun • Tom Chan • Caleb Chan

about doing something for both education and the community of British Columbia.' That's why we zeroed in on this concert hall."

Anyone who meets Caleb or Tom Chan cannot help but experience their decorous modesty. Warm, but impeccably polite, their self-effacing manner stands in stark contrast to the size and scope of the international business enterprises they lead. As business leaders and philanthropists, they work as hard on keeping a low profile as they do on accomplishing their agenda. A 1985 Newsweek article referred to the Chan family as among 'The Oriental Rothschilds'. Devout Christians who have financially supported their Church's Canadian expansion, their modesty springs from deeply-held religious and philosophical beliefs as well as from prizing their privacy.

The Chan family's aversion to publicity led them to initially insist that their donation to the University of British Columbia be anonymous. Only upon being persuaded by President David Strangway of the university's exigency to publicize their gift in order to claim a matching government grant did the Chans finally relent.[11] Even then, they were reticent about the limelight, expressing concern about the monetary value of their gift overshadowing the values that compelled them to give, especially the Chan brothers' desire through the gift to honor their father, Chan Shun.[12] That philosophy is, perhaps, best captured in a moving speech Tom Chan delivered during the Chan Centre's formal May 1997 opening night ceremonies – a story told, father to sons, repeatedly. (See quote above)

Chan Shun's philanthropic influence extended well beyond his sons. When the Chan Centre gift became public, then-Lieutenant Governor David Lam – who is renown both for his generosity[13] and his encouragement of philanthropy by the Chinese-Canadian community[14] – credited Chan as "the single most important person in influencing my attitude of giving." The friendship between the two Chinese immigrants was proving to have a profound impact on Canadian philanthropy. As early as 1985, Lam's charitable giving was already reported to be $5 Million per year.[15]

Chan Shun's origins were simple and humble. He escaped communist China when he was in his late twenties, journeying across Asia in a tribulation-filled search for some opportunity. Finally, he arrived in Hong Kong with a modest grubstake. Deprived of formal education, he worked his way up from sewing in a T-shirt factory to head an international business conglomerate with interests in real estate and clothing manufacturing, principally Crocodile Garments Ltd.

The philosophy of giving early, often, and selflessly to one's community is one that is best learned by example. Indeed, it was both Chan Shun's words and example, as carried forward by his sons, that led them to honor their father – not only by naming a concert hall after him, but by continuing his legacy of stewardship. And while the Chan Centre for the Performing Arts stands to honor a beloved father, it also stands as a monument to Tom Chan's charitable philosophy, one without which many performing arts centres throughout North America might not exist: "We are responsible for passing on good things and better opportunities to the next generation."

Chan Shun's lessons to his sons were not limited to charity. Demonstrating business acumen like their father, after assuming control, both Tom and Caleb Chan have created flourishing international enterprises that have expanded their father's legacy.

As Chan Shun predicted, Strangway would not be disappointed. With the Chan family's help, Vancouver and UBC would have its new performing arts centre. A need that Strangway, himself, didn't begin to understand, at the time, would be fulfilled.

"It's as if it has been here all along", Strangway pronounced, "It was immediately a significant part of the life of the campus. This does not always happen when you open new building on campus. It takes time. It is almost as if there was a hole and the hole had to be filled. Having filled the hole, it did even more than people envisioned. It succeeded far beyond my wildest dreams."

The main entry from the forecourt

OPENING NIGHT

There were plenty of white-knuckle concerns over the Chan Centre's development, but nothing compared to one dread fear: Chan Shun – the Centre's namesake – might not live long enough to see the Centre opened.

"Tom's father was quite ill", Bing Thom murmured. "We raced to finish the building."

"Father's health was going downhill quite fast", Tom Chan said. "We anticipated a grand opening that would introduce the hall to the community, but we feared he might not last that long."

Finally the concern became unbearable. The university resolved to have a special early opening to honor Chan Shun and the pace picked up yet again.

The university was determined that its own students give the Centre's inaugural performance to underscore its commitment to giving its students a wonderful performance facility.

When opening night arrived, the Centre was only 92% complete. Chorus wagons stood unfinished, concealed behind pinned-up fabric. The Centre's fire systems were uncommissioned so a fire truck and its crew stood watch outside. Hurriedly, the concert hall seating was just being installed that afternoon.

"As you know", Don Paterson explained, "the seats are the last thing put into a concert hall. They had been manufactured in a plant in Michigan, and were being sent to Vancouver in three huge articulated trucks. We knew that the hall was incapable of receiving all three trucks at one time so the trucks were scheduled to leave Michigan eighteen hours apart. Each would be off-loaded and removed before the next one arrived." Then winter intervened.

"A severe snowstorm came down through the Midwest", said Paterson. "Truck number two skidded off the road in Iowa. The cab was damaged but the truck wasn't. Meanwhile, truck number three was rerouted all the way south to Colorado to avoid the snowstorm. All this happened in the middle of a very tight schedule to accomplish the Chan Shun opening on time."

The trucking company found another less powerful cab to replace the damaged one, but it could not pull the truck at full highway speed. The load limped all the way to Calgary where a fully-powered cab waited to continue to the trek to Vancouver Eventually, Murphy's Law played out and all three trucks arrived at once. Pandemonium ensued. Paterson remembers someone turning to him and asking, "What do we do now?"

"Nothing in life has prepared me to give you an answer to that question", Paterson replied laughing, "There was nothing else to do but laugh at that point."

The forest lighting system that was so integral to bringing the forest inside the lobby had not yet been installed, either. Earlier that day, BTA staffers trekked to Home Depot® to purchase backyard party floodlights mounted on stakes. Several of the firm's architects, including Bing Thom, himself, crawled around the forest floor, running extension cords, and focusing lights so that the stately old forest would be visible from the lobby that evening.

Paterson had spent the two previous days frantically trying to secure an occupancy permit from university officials so that the ceremonies could occur. Incredulous, he discovered that planning and permit officials had not even started the process. As by-the-book types are wont to do, they resisted Paterson's entreaties to make exceptions. Once again, Paterson trotted to the President's office, bureaucrat-weary but determined.

By three o'clock that afternoon, the permit still had not been granted. Paterson's stomach knotted and boiled, worrying that some sixteen hundred people would be making their way to the celebration only hours later, finding red faces and padlocked doors. Finally, at the last minute, a temporary occupancy permit was begrudgingly granted.

The show would go on.

In the early afternoon, so tired he couldn't summon a smile, Chan Shun told his son Tom that he didn't want to attend the opening. Tom Chan insisted he summon the strength to accompany his family.

Bing Thom and James Fankhauser • (next page) Bing Thom and Tom Chan

Feeble but smiling, with oxygen at the ready, Chan Shun was wheeled into the hall, surrounded by his family and friends.

"We sat up there in one of the balconies looking down over it all", said Strangway. "It was actually very emotional because we had all lived through a lot of trials and tribulations and trade-offs, and finally, we sat there realizing that it had all been worth it."

Usually, the first notes sounded before an audience in a hall's inaugural performance are made by musicians. This time, two architects performed first: the first its principal donor and the second its principal architect. Tom Chan, like Bing Thom, is a University of California-Berkeley-trained architect; he sounded the gong. Then, Bing Thom conducted *Oh Canada*.

Tap, tap. The university orchestra's concertmaster drew the other musicians' attention. An oboe sounded and the traditional cacaphonous utterings of violins, violas, cellos, and basses resolved into sweet consonance. Subtle coughs sounded as voices cleared. Conductor James Fankhauser strode on stage as applause swelled. The 100-piece orchestra and 300-voice chorus launched into the world premier performance of a choral-orchestral work by Srul Irving Glick, commissioned for the Centre's inaugural concert: *The Hour Has Come*.

The hall's acoustical depths were fully plumbed that evening. Following the premier, *Mozart's Concerto in E-flat* for two pianos was performed by pianists Robert Silverman and Jane Coop, accompanied by an able university orchestra conducted by Jesse Read. Finally, the splendidly moving Beethoven's *Ninth Symphony* capped the inaugural performance. "The first note of music was such a thrill", Don Paterson remembered. "It was quite clear to the acousticians and to the architects that the acoustics were even better than they had imagined they would be."

"When we finally had the chance to recognize him", David Strangway recalled, "and ask him to stand, the whole audience just stood and clapped and clapped and clapped, not just for the concert hall but for Chan Shun. He didn't live very long after that. It was one of my greatest satisfactions that he could be there to actually see the opening happen."

Following Tom Chan's opening night speech from the Concert Hall stage, the audience burst forth with a thundering standing ovation. With characteristic deference, Chan slowly lifted his outstretched arm up in a sweeping arc, stopping when his hand pointed to his father in the balcony above.

From his seat in the audience, Chan Shun smiled, nodded and gazed at the gleaming faces and gazes fixed upon him. This rarely emotional man, obviously moved, feebly spoke his last public words: "This is my dream come true."

NOTES

1   William Blake, Letter, August 23, 1799 (published in The Letters of
    William Blake, 1956)

2   The Vancouver Sun, April 27, 1997

3   Henrik Ibsen, Hilde, in The Master Builder, act 3

4   Artur Schnabel, Quoted in: Chicago Daily News, June 11, 1958

5   Lloyd Dykk, Chan Centre's first trial – Job – proves a winner, The Vancouver Sun,
    May 12, 1997

6   Fred Gilpin, Chan Centre for the Performing Arts, Canadian Business and Current
    Affairs, April 1988

7   Lloyd Dykk, Size matters in triumphant version of Vespers of 1610: The intimate
    confines of the Chan Centre enable a small chorus to demonstrate an
    astonishing range of expression in Monteverdi's eclectic work, Vancouver Sun,
    August 8, 2000

8   E B White, "The Old and the New," in New Yorker, June 19, 1937; repr. in Writings
    from the New Yorker 1927-76, edited by Rebecca Dale, 1991

9   Doug Ward and Gillian Shaw, They wield power and influence in the province
    where we live and will affect its direction during the next year. The Sun looks at
    BC's newsmakers of '98, The Vancouver Sun, January 2, 1998

10 Tom Chan, Opening Night Ceremonies Speech, May 12, 1997, Courtesy of
    Tom Chan

11 Robert Matas, Responding to Resentment, The Globe and Mail, July 7, 1990

12 Peter C Newman, The Bamboo Network; Vancouver's Chinese Establishment,
    The Vancouver Sun, Saturday October 31, 1998

13 The Vancouver Sun, Friday, Brothers identified as big UBC donors,
    November 24, 1989

14 Peter C Newman, The Bamboo Network; Vancouver's Chinese Establishment,
    The Vancouver Sun, Saturday October 31, 1998

15 Peter C Newman, The Bamboo Network; Vancouver's Chinese Establishment,
    The Vancouver Sun, Saturday October 31, 1998

ACKNOWLEDGEMENTS

(in addition to the consultant team)

Joyce Hinton, UBC

Bob Kubicek, UBC

Michael Noon, UBC

Don Paterson, UBC

Dennis Pavelich, UBC

Martha Piper, UBC

Jesse Read, UBC

Rheinzink Canada

David Strangway

FACT SHEET

Project	Chan Centre for the Performing Arts
Client/Project Managers	University of British Columbia (UBC)
Architect	Bing Thom Architects
	Bing Thom
	Michael Heeney
	Luciano Zago
	Arno Matis
	Earle Briggs
	Lynn Pilon
	Ben Chin
	Scott Baldwin
	Shinobu Homma
	Ralf Janus
	Neil Kaye
	Michael Lui
	Judith MacDougal
	Caroline Munk
	Bonnie Thom
	Deanna Yue
Acoustical Consultant	ARTEC
Theatre Consultant	Theatre Projects, Inc
Cost Consultants	Donnell Cost Consultants
	James Vermullen
	Hanscomb Ltd
Structural Engineer	CY Loh & Associates Ltd
Electrical Engineer	Reid Crowther & Partners
Mechanical Engineer	Yoneda & Associates Ltd
Code Consultant	Locke MacKinnon Domingo & Gibson
Lighting	Lam Consultants
Landscape Architects	Cornellia Oberlander
	Elizabeth Watts
Construction	Ellis Don Construction

NEILL ARCHER ROAN

Neill Archer Roan is principal and CEO of The Roan Group, a consulting firm based in Washington, DC. A former concert musician, university professor, performing arts center executive, and producer, Roan appears frequently throughout North America presenting seminars, keynote addresses, and workshops. An award-winning art director, Roan's branding and marketing campaigns for nonprofits have garnered over 100 national and international awards.

COLOPHON

© 2002 Black Dog Publishing Ltd and Bing Thom Architects
ISBN 1 901033481

DESIGN
Rhonda McNaught, Kaldor Design Group Ltd

PRODUCTION ASSISTANCE
Gary Blakeley

PHOTOGRAPHY
Holly Chan 38
Tom Chan 69
Daryl Kahn Cline 16, 18, 19, 42, 44, 74, 75, 78, 81.1, 83, 91, 93
Anthony Buckley & Constantine of London 87.1
Couvrette/Ottawa 80.2
Martin Dee, UBC ITServices 80.1
Tim Matheson 54
Tim Richmond 81.4
Dave Roels 81.2
Steve J. Sherman 81.3
Martin Tessler cover, 4, 9, 11, 13, 14, 15, 20, 22, 25, 26, 30, 32, 36, 39, 40, 41, 43, 45, 46, 47, 49, 50, 52, 53, 55, 58, 59, 60, 62, 67, 70, 73, 76, 77, 84, 87.2, 87.3, 89
Wayne Thom 65
Waite Air Photos Inc 35

PRINTED IN CHINA

British Library cataloguing-in-publication data. A catalogue record is available from the British Library.

Black Dog Publishing Limited
5 Ravenscroft Street
London E2 7SH